Scott Foresman Reading

Practice Book

Scott Foresman

Editorial Offices: Glenview, Illinois • Parsippany, New Jersey • New York, New York
Sales Offices: Parsippany, New Jersey • Duluth, Georgia • Glenview, Illinois
Coppell, Texas • Ontario, California

Illustration Credits

Teresa Anderko: pp. 2, 88, 118; **Nelle Davis:** pp. 52, 57, 58, 72, 78; **Waldo Dunn:** pp. 12, 18, 42, 148; **Martin Jenkins:** p. 53; **Vickie Learner:** pp. 122, 128; **Mapping Specialists:** p. 30; **Laurie O'Keefe:** p. 130; **TSI Graphics:** pp. 20, 40, 50, 100, 140, 150; **N. Jo Tufts:** p. 7; **Jessica Wolk-Stanley:** pp. 8, 22, 32, 102.

ISBN: 0-328-02246-2
ISBN: 0-328-04050-9

8 9 10 V011 10 09 08 07 06 05 04
7 8 9 10 V011 10 09 08 07 06 05 04

Table of Contents

Unit 2

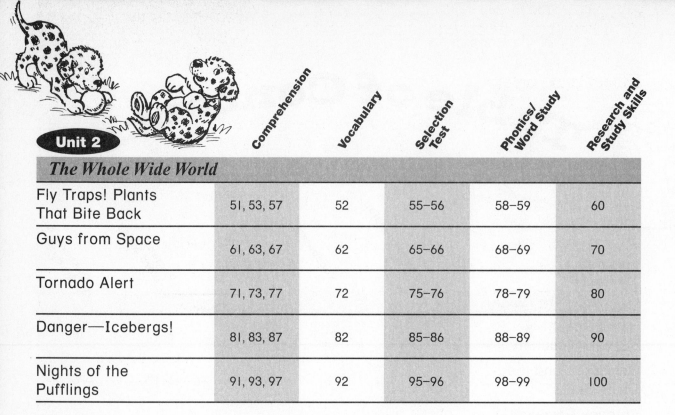

The Whole Wide World	Comprehension	Vocabulary	Selection Test	Phonics/ Word Study	Research and Study Skills
Fly Traps! Plants That Bite Back	51, 53, 57	52	55–56	58–59	60
Guys from Space	61, 63, 67	62	65–66	68–69	70
Tornado Alert	71, 73, 77	72	75–76	78–79	80
Danger—Icebergs!	81, 83, 87	82	85–86	88–89	90
Nights of the Pufflings	91, 93, 97	92	95–96	98–99	100

Unit 3

Getting the Job Done	Comprehension	Vocabulary	Selection Test	Phonics/ Word Study	Research and Study Skills
What Do Authors Do?	101, 103, 107	102	105–106	108–109	110
Tops and Bottoms	111, 113, 117	112	115–116	118–119	120
Mom's Best Friend	121, 123, 127	122	125–126	128–129	130
Brave as a Mountain Lion	131, 133, 137	132	135–136	138–139	140
Your Dad Was Just Like You	141, 143, 147	142	145–146	148–149	150

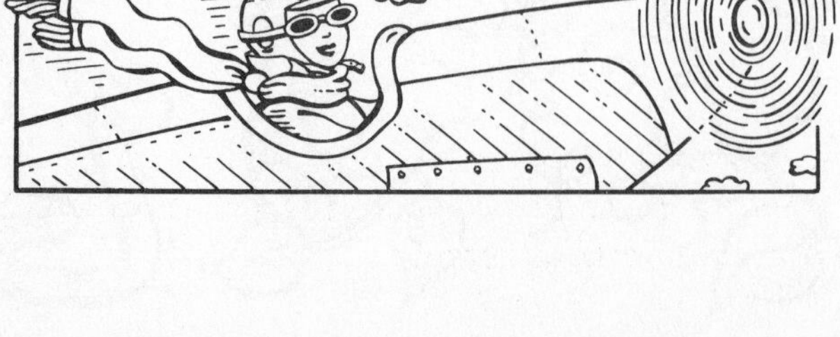

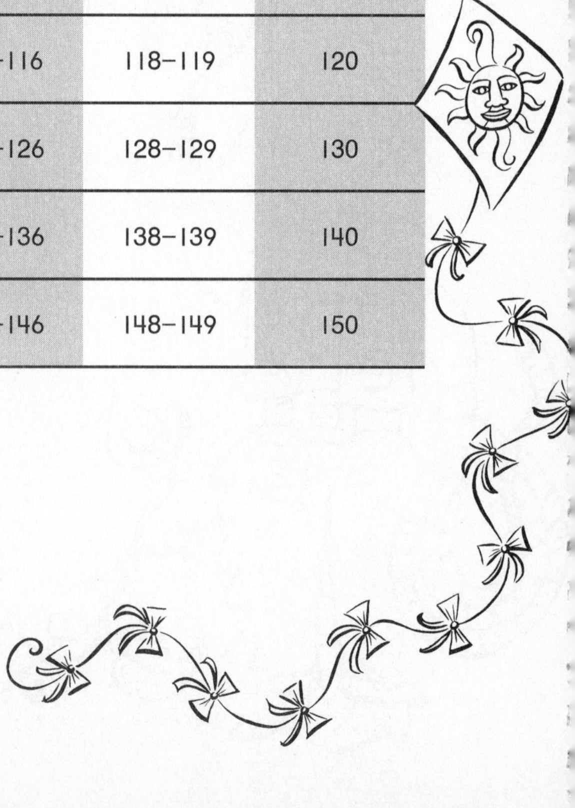

Name ______________________________

Sequence

- **Sequence** is the order in which things happen in a story.
- Clue words, such as *before* and *after,* can tell you when something happens.

Before → **Next** → **Last**

Directions: Reread "First Day at Camp." Write the story events from the box in the flow chart in the order that they happen. Two have been done for you.

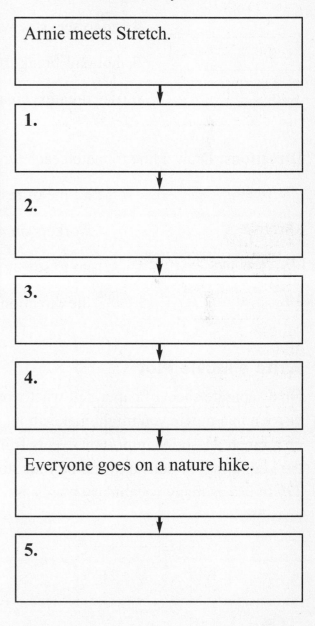

Story Events
Arnie holds a snake.
Everyone hikes to the cabin.
Everyone takes a nap.
Everyone eats lunch.
Arnie thinks of his mom and Louanne.
Arnie meets Stretch.
Everyone goes on a nature hike.

Arnie meets Stretch.

↓

1.

↓

2.

↓

3.

↓

4.

↓

Everyone goes on a nature hike.

↓

5.

Notes for Home: Your child read a story and then identified the order in which the story events occurred. ***Home Activity:*** Read a story with your child. Encourage him or her to retell the story with the events in the appropriate sequence.

Name ______________________________________

Vocabulary

Directions: Write the word from the box that belongs in each group.

Check the Words You Know
__ cowboys
__ imagination
__ summer
__ vacation
__ visit
__ west

_______________ **1.** spring, winter, __________

_______________ **2.** ranch workers, people who tend cattle, __________

_______________ **3.** north, east, __________

_______________ **4.** go to see, stay with, __________

_______________ **5.** holiday, break from work, __________

_______________ **6.** day dreams, creative thinking, __________

Directions: Draw a line to match each word with its definition.

7. west	a time of rest from school or work
8. visit	workers on a cattle ranch
9. cowboys	go to see
10. vacation	the direction opposite of east

Write a Movie Plot

On a separate sheet of paper, tell what would happen in a movie you might make about life on a ranch. Describe important events from the beginning, middle, and end of your story. Try to use as many vocabulary words as possible.

Notes for Home: Your child identified and used vocabulary words from *How I Spent My Summer Vacation.* ***Home Activity:*** With your child, look at a picture book about the Old West. Discuss what it would be like to live there, using as many vocabulary words as you can.

Name ______________________________________

Sequence

- **Sequence** is the order in which things happen in a story.
- Clue words, such as *before* and *after,* can tell you when something happens.

Directions: Reread what happens in *How I Spent My Summer Vacation* when Wallace is captured. Then answer the questions below.

But suddenly I noticed a terrible sight.
The cattle were stirring and stamping with fright.
It's a scene I'll remember to my very last day.
"They're gonna stampede!" I heard somebody say.
Just then they came charging. They charged right at *me!*
I looked for a hiding place—
a rock, or a tree.
What I found was a tablecloth spread out on the ground.
So I turned like a matador
And spun it around.
It was a new kind of cowboying, a fantastic display!
The cattle were frightened and stampeded . . . away.

1. What terrible sight does Wallace notice? ______________________

____

2. What is the very first thing Wallace does after the cattle charge at him?

____

3. What does Wallace do after he picks up the tablecloth? __________

____

4. What is the last thing that happens in the passage? _____________

____

5. On a separate sheet of paper, tell what happens to Wallace on his way to Aunt Fern's house. Describe the events in the order in which they happen.

Notes for Home: Your child read a story and then identified the order in which its events took place. ***Home Activity:*** Work with your child to write a description of a family member doing a chore. Be sure to describe the steps in the order that they are done.

Test-Taking Tips

1. Write your name on the test.
2. Read the directions carefully. Make sure you know exactly what you are supposed to do.
3. Read the question twice. Make sure you understand what the question is asking.
4. Read the answer choices for the question. Eliminate choices that do not make sense.
5. Mark your answer carefully.
6. Check your answer. Make sure that it makes the most sense out of all the answer choices.
7. If you have difficulty answering a question, you may want to go on to the next question. You can come back to difficult questions later.
8. If you finish the test early, go back and check all your answers.

Name ______________________________

Selection Test

Directions: Choose the best answer to each item. Mark the space for the answer you have chosen.

Part 1: Vocabulary

Find the answer choice that means about the same as the underlined word in each sentence.

1. Joe met three <u>cowboys</u>.
- ⬭ animals with four legs
- ⬭ workers at a cattle ranch
- ⬭ boys who go to school
- ⬭ farmers who grow corn

2. Lita will <u>visit</u> Aunt Sally.
- ⬭ call on the phone
- ⬭ have dinner with
- ⬭ send a letter to
- ⬭ go to see

3. Ray lives out <u>west</u>.
- ⬭ the direction of sunset
- ⬭ in a large house
- ⬭ on a ranch
- ⬭ very far from here

4. She has a great <u>imagination</u>.
- ⬭ silly idea
- ⬭ knowing how to make up things in the mind
- ⬭ kind of house
- ⬭ chance to see some interesting places

5. When does <u>summer</u> begin?
- ⬭ season before fall
- ⬭ time when children go to school
- ⬭ season between fall and winter
- ⬭ time for taking care of cattle

6. Our <u>vacation</u> lasted one week.
- ⬭ long trip
- ⬭ time away from school, home, or business
- ⬭ easy job
- ⬭ place to stay away from home

Part 2: Comprehension

Use what you know about the story to answer each item.

7. Wallace went out west to—
- ⬭ become a cowboy.
- ⬭ learn to ride a horse.
- ⬭ go to a new school.
- ⬭ visit Aunt Fern.

8. Where is Wallace when he tells his story?
- ⬭ on a train
- ⬭ in school
- ⬭ on the plains
- ⬭ at a ranch

GO ON

Name ______________________________

9. In Wallace's story, what happened to him first?
   - He learned to ride a horse.
   - Aunt Fern called him.
   - He was captured by cowboys.
   - He became a cowhand.

10. When did Wallace finally get to Aunt Fern's house?
   - after the barbecue
   - after the stampede
   - after the roundup
   - after the band played

11. Why did the cowboys say that Kid Bleff was a "true buckaroo"?
   - He rode a horse.
   - He stopped the stampede.
   - He knew how to dance.
   - He liked barbecues.

12. What can you tell about cowboys from this story?
   - They make a lot of money.
   - They work hard.
   - They never have any fun.
   - They are good singers.

13. What does Wallace's teacher think about him?
   - She thinks he is very brave.
   - She feels sorry about what happened to him.
   - She thinks he is very smart.
   - She does not believe his story is true.

14. What part of Wallace's story most likely happened?
   - He was captured by cowboys.
   - He worked on a cattle roundup.
   - He visited Aunt Fern.
   - He stopped a stampede.

15. His parents probably think that Wallace—
   - had a great vacation.
   - still has a wild imagination.
   - got the rest he needed.
   - will bring a cow to school.

STOP

Name ______________________________________

Drawing Conclusions

REVIEW

Directions: Read the story. Then read each question about the story. Choose the best answer to the question. Mark the space for the answer you have chosen.

Cows on the Loose

"Look! There's another one!" Luis yelled to his dad. He pointed to a break in the fence. The wire had snapped and the ends hung down.

Not too far away, three cows were resting under a tree. "Those cows have our brand on them," said Luis. "I'll round them up." Luis circled the cows and rode up behind them. "Get going!" he shouted.

Trapper barked until they had trotted back through the break in the fence.

Dad jumped down from his horse. He had his tools out and he was uncoiling the fence wire he had brought. "We have only a mile of fence to go," he said. "We'll be done in an hour."

1. Luis and his father were out to—
- find cows without brands.
- look for a lost cow.
- check the fence for breaks.
- collect a roll of fence wire.

2. The three cows—
- belong to another rancher.
- are always running away.
- are always breaking the fence.
- belong to Luis's family.

3. They drive the cows back through the break in the fence because
- the cows are on someone else's land.
- the cows belong to someone they know.
- they need to brand them.
- whoever finds the cows gets to keep them.

4. Trapper is—
- a horse.
- a dog.
- Luis's nickname for his dad.
- one of the three cows.

5. Luis's dad was carrying tools and wire because—
- he always liked to have them handy.
- Luis had told him to bring them along.
- he'd been building a fence.
- he expected to find breaks in the fence to fix.

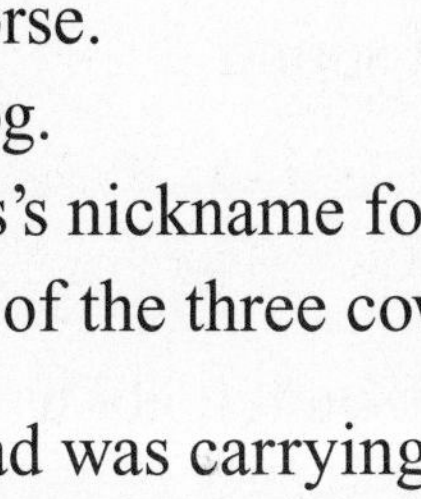

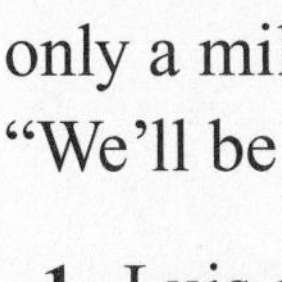

Notes for Home: Your child has used story details and what he or she already knows to draw conclusions. ***Home Activity:*** Watch a nature show or video with your child. Pause to ask him or her questions that will require drawing conclusions about what the animals are doing and why.

Name ______________________________

Phonics: Short Vowels

Directions: Choose the word with the short vowel sound to complete each sentence. Write the word on the line.

_______________ **1.** My parents thought we all needed to (relax/sleep).

_______________ **2.** So, my whole family took a (vacation/trip).

_______________ **3.** We went (west/east) to a ranch.

_______________ **4.** I rode horses on the (easy/rough) trails.

_______________ **5.** I saw a huge (cactus/snake).

_______________ **6.** That was the best (summer/week) ever.

Directions: Circle the word that has the short vowel sound. Then underline the letter or letters in the word that stand for that vowel sound.

7. not	you	so
8. sleep	stamp	stoop
9. neat	next	nice
10. queen	quiet	quit
11. head	heed	home
12. spoon	spent	speed
13. reek	road	rocks
14. same	saddle	safe
15. stand	steep	stool

Notes for Home: Your child reviewed words with short vowel sounds, such as *hat, best, lip, pot,* or *sun.* ***Home Activity:*** Say each of these words aloud and listen for its vowel sound. Work with your child to list other words with *a, e, i, o,* and *u* that have the same vowel sounds.

Name ____________________________________

Phonics: Inflected Endings

REVIEW

Directions: Read the underlined word in each sentence. Choose the word that has the same ending sound **and** the same number of syllables as the underlined word. Mark the space for the answer you have chosen.

1. Mike carried his books in his pack.
- ⬭ worried
- ⬭ spent
- ⬭ played
- ⬭ dragged

2. Dad was making popcorn.
- ⬭ along
- ⬭ thinking
- ⬭ capturing
- ⬭ bring

3. The batter missed the ball.
- ⬭ promised
- ⬭ seed
- ⬭ passed
- ⬭ headed

4. Eric was smiling at his dad.
- ⬭ stampeding
- ⬭ remembering
- ⬭ sting
- ⬭ driving

5. The cat batted the toy mouse.
- ⬭ past
- ⬭ knotted
- ⬭ crossed
- ⬭ zipped

6. Carrie was riding on a horse.
- ⬭ borrowing
- ⬭ swing
- ⬭ going
- ⬭ ridden

7. Lynda's team was winning.
- ⬭ wing
- ⬭ beginning
- ⬭ grinning
- ⬭ wins

8. Ted and Adam traded lunches.
- ⬭ made
- ⬭ played
- ⬭ braided
- ⬭ feed

9. We stayed in the bus.
- ⬭ made
- ⬭ fast
- ⬭ headed
- ⬭ staying

10. She is visiting her aunt.
- ⬭ stopping
- ⬭ picking
- ⬭ ring
- ⬭ forgetting

Notes for Home: Your child read words with *-ed* and *-ing* endings and listened for the number of syllables in each word. ***Home Activity:*** Read a story with your child and look for words with *-ing* and *-ed* endings. Have your child read these words aloud.

Name ______________________________

Parts of a Book

Books have different parts that help you find the information you need. A **table of contents** lists chapters, articles or stories, and their page numbers. An **index** lists subjects that the book covers and tells the page on which the information can be found. It is usually in the back of the book.

Directions: Use the table of contents and the index to answer the questions.

Table of Contents

Washington D.C.

Chapter 1
Sights and Museums 3

Chapter 2
Parks and Recreation 15

Chapter 3
Performing Arts 33

Chapter 4
Seasonal Events 39

Index

Children's Theatre, 34
Constitution Gardens, 15
Festivals
  Cherry Blossom, 41
  Kite, 49
Hirshhorn Sculpture Garden, 4
National Aquarium, 5
National Gallery of Art, 8
Rock Creek Park, 17
Smithsonian Information Center, 11
Youth Orchestra, 38

1. In which chapter would you look if you wanted to see a dance performance while on summer vacation in Washington D.C.?

____

2. On what page would you start reading if you knew you wanted to spend your summer vacation hiking? What place for hiking will be discussed in that chapter?

____

3. In which chapter would you look to find out what special activities happen in the summer? Which festivals might you be able to see?

____

4. On what page is there information about the National Aquarium? __________

5. On what page is there information about the Children's Theatre? __________

Notes for Home: Your child used a table of contents and index to answer questions. ***Home Activity:*** Look at a table of contents and index from a favorite book. Have your child use the book parts to locate specific information.

Name ____________________________________

Drawing Conclusions

- A **conclusion** is a decision you make about what happens in a story.
- You **draw conclusions** when you use what you know to make decisions that make sense about characters or events.

Directions: Reread "Spider's Story." Then complete the table. Write a conclusion for the evidence given. Write evidence that supports each conclusion given.

Evidence (Story Details and What I Already Know)	Conclusion
1.	The chicken didn't mean to go to the part of town where foxes live.
The bad part of town is the part where foxes live.	2.
3.	The chicken is nervous about being in this part of town.
4.	
The fox is hungry, and foxes eat chickens.	5.

Notes for Home: Your child read a story and drew conclusions from its details. ***Home Activity:*** Have your child tell you about things that he or she saw on the way home. Ask your child to draw conclusions. *(Why do you think the moving van is in front of the blue house?)*

Name ________________________________

Vocabulary

Directions: Choose the word from the box that best completes each sentence. Write the word on the line to the left.

Check the Words You Know
__ breakfast
__ comfortable
__ cozy
__ forest
__ gobbled
__ hungry
__ promise

______________ **1.** My big brother is always _____, so he eats all the time.

______________ **2.** He eats a huge _____ every morning.

______________ **3.** This morning he _____ it down in about a minute.

Directions: Choose the word from the box that best matches each clue. Write the word on the line.

______________ **4.** snug and warm

______________ **5.** ate quickly

______________ **6.** a large area with many trees

______________ **7.** the meal before lunch

______________ **8.** how you might feel before dinner

______________ **9.** having comfort

______________ **10.** give your word

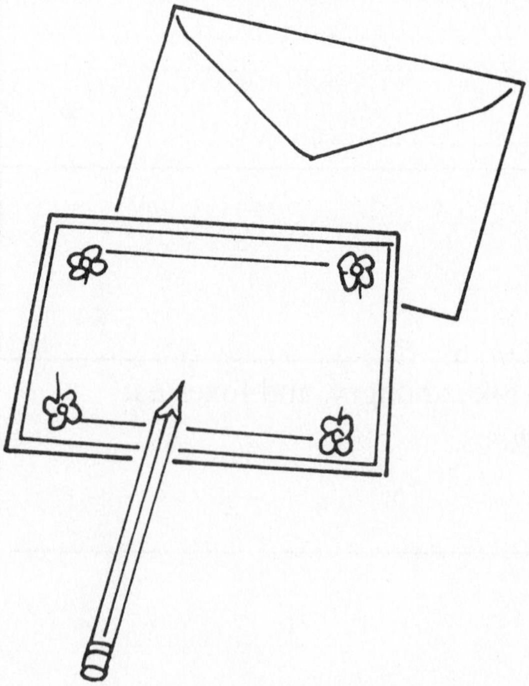

Write a Thank-You Note

Think of the last time you visited a friend, a neighbor, or a family member at his or her house. On a separate sheet of paper, write a thank-you note to the people you visited. Remember to thank your host for any meals that you shared. Use as many vocabulary words as you can.

Notes for Home: Your child identified and used vocabulary words from *Goldilocks and the Three Bears*. ***Home Activity:*** Ask your child to tell you about having good manners. Encourage your child to use as many vocabulary words as possible.

Name ____________________

Drawing Conclusions

- A **conclusion** is a decision you make about what happens in a story.
- You **draw conclusions** when you use what you know to make decisions that make sense about characters or events.

Directions: Reread what happens in *Goldilocks and the Three Bears* when the three bears sit down to breakfast. Then answer the questions below.

"Patooie!" cried big old Papa Bear. "This porridge is scalding! I've burned my tongue!"

"I'm dying!" cried Baby Bear.

"Now really," said Mama Bear, who was of medium size. "That's quite enough."

"I know," said Papa Bear. "Why don't we go for a spin while the porridge is cooling?"

"Excellent," said Mama Bear. So they got on their rusty old bicycle and off they went.

1. Why do you think Baby Bear says he is dying?

____

2. Who do you think Mama Bear is talking to when she says, "That's quite enough"? What do you think she means?

____

____

3. Did the bears plan to be away from home long? How do you know?

____

4. Did the fuss over the porridge put Mama Bear in a bad mood? Explain.

____

5. On a separate sheet of paper, draw a conclusion about Goldilocks. Give examples from the story.

Notes for Home: Your child read a story and used details to draw some conclusions about its characters. ***Home Activity:*** Read a story with your child. Ask your child to draw conclusions about why the characters act the way they they do.

Test-Taking Tips

1. Write your name on the test.
2. Read the directions carefully. Make sure you know exactly what you are supposed to do.
3. Read the question twice. Make sure you understand what the question is asking.
4. Read the answer choices for the question. Eliminate choices that do not make sense.
5. Mark your answer carefully.
6. Check your answer. Make sure that it makes the most sense out of all the answer choices.
7. If you have difficulty answering a question, you may want to go on to the next question. You can come back to difficult questions later.
8. If you finish the test early, go back and check all your answers.

Selection Test

Directions: Choose the best answer to each item. Mark the space for the answer you have chosen.

Part 1: Vocabulary

Find the answer choice that means about the same as the underlined word in each sentence.

1. She had a big <u>breakfast</u>.
- ⬭ a long sleep
- ⬭ the first meal of the day
- ⬭ a large coat
- ⬭ loud noise heard at night

2. Theo walked through the <u>forest</u>.
- ⬭ place where many trees grow
- ⬭ large store
- ⬭ wall made of small stones
- ⬭ high fence

3. I <u>promise</u> to be home soon.
- ⬭ want
- ⬭ really hope
- ⬭ think
- ⬭ give one's word

4. We are all <u>hungry</u>.
- ⬭ tired and sleepy
- ⬭ in need of rest
- ⬭ feeling a need for food
- ⬭ happy and excited

5. This is a <u>cozy</u> room.
- ⬭ warm and snug
- ⬭ large
- ⬭ filled with things
- ⬭ small

6. Jon <u>gobbled</u> his lunch.
- ⬭ did not like
- ⬭ warmed up
- ⬭ made with care
- ⬭ ate fast

7. That is a <u>comfortable</u> chair.
- ⬭ of a red color
- ⬭ giving an easy feeling
- ⬭ made of wood
- ⬭ costing a lot of money

Part 2: Comprehension

Use what you know about the story to answer each item.

8. Goldilocks's mother asked her to—
- ⬭ go to the forest.
- ⬭ visit the bears' house.
- ⬭ buy some muffins.
- ⬭ get some milk.

GO ON

9. What happened first in this story?
- ⬭ The bears went for a ride.
- ⬭ Goldilocks ate some porridge.
- ⬭ The bears sat down for breakfast.
- ⬭ Goldilocks broke a chair.

10. When Goldilocks found brown fur in the house, she—
- ⬭ thought cats lived there.
- ⬭ knew it was the bears' house.
- ⬭ cleaned the house.
- ⬭ left the house fast.

11. What did Goldilocks do just after she ate the porridge?
- ⬭ took a nap
- ⬭ sat in a chair
- ⬭ walked through the forest
- ⬭ met the three bears

12. What can you tell about Goldilocks from this story?
- ⬭ She has many friends.
- ⬭ She does not like porridge.
- ⬭ She loves bears.
- ⬭ She often gets into trouble.

13. How did the bears feel when they found that someone had been eating their porridge?
- ⬭ tired
- ⬭ excited
- ⬭ pleased
- ⬭ surprised

14. What part of this story could **not** really happen?
- ⬭ A girl eats porridge.
- ⬭ Three bears talk.
- ⬭ A girl takes a nap.
- ⬭ Three bears eat some food.

15. What rule does Goldilocks most need to learn?
- ⬭ Don't talk to people you don't know.
- ⬭ Always say "please."
- ⬭ Don't take things that do not belong to you.
- ⬭ Think before you talk.

STOP

Name ______________________________

Cause and Effect

REVIEW

Directions: Read the story. Then read each question about the story. Choose the best answer to the question. Mark the space for the answer you have chosen.

One Really Bad Day

"There is nothing to do here," yawned Goldy. Then she saw a cuckoo clock on the wall. It might be fun to get that down and take it apart. She stood on a stool to take it down. Suddenly she slipped and fell off the stool, dropping the clock.

When the clock hit the floor, a wooden bird darted out and cried, "Cuckoo, cuckoo, cuckoo!" Because of the noise, the dog woke up and began to bark loudly.

The barking startled Goldy so much that she fell backwards into the rocker. The rocker tipped back, rocking over the tail of the cat. The cat yowled and jumped into the air. It leaped to the top of the sofa and then on to Goldy's back. It hung on tight with its claws.

1. Goldy was bored, so she—
- started to rock.
- woke up the dog.
- played with the cat.
- decided to take apart the clock.

2. What made the cuckoo come out of the clock?
- Goldy dropped the clock.
- It was two o'clock.
- Goldy had the clock in her hands.
- Goldy took the clock apart.

3. What did the dog's bark cause to happen?
- Goldy dropped the clock.
- The cat woke up and yowled.
- Goldy fell backwards into the rocker.
- Goldy fell off the stool.

4. What made the cat jump into the air?
- It heard the cuckoo.
- It heard the dog bark.
- The rocker went over its tail.
- Goldy tripped over it.

5. Which word in the second paragraph signals a cause-effect relationship?
- cuckoo
- because
- loud
- woke

Notes for Home: Your child identified causes and effects in a story. ***Home Activity:*** Make up *if-then* statements with your child. One person uses *if* to describe a possible event, and the other person uses *then* to tell what might happen as a result.

Name ____________________

Phonics: Double Consonants

Directions: Choose the word in the box that best completes each sentence. Add the missing letter and write the word on the line to the left.

excel_ent	gob_led	ha_py	li_tle	por_idge

__________ **1.** Papa Bear: I am _____ to be back home.

__________ **2.** Baby Bear: I am a _____ tired from our long bike ride.

__________ **3.** Mama Bear: Let's eat our _____ now.

__________ **4.** Papa Bear: What an _____ idea! I'm very hungry!

__________ **5.** Baby Bear: Oh, look! Someone has _____ up my breakfast.

Directions: Say the name of each picture. Write the missing letters to complete each word.

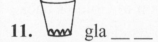

6. 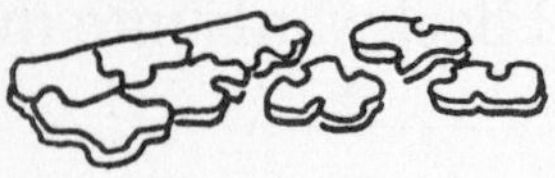 pu __ __ le

7.  she __ __

8. 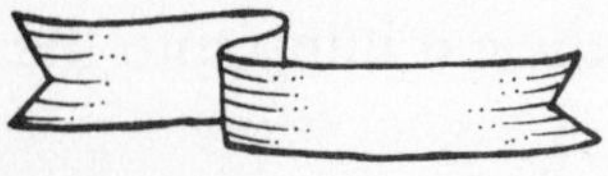 ri __ __ on

9.  zi __ __ er

10.  pe __ __ y

11.  gla __ __

12.  ha __ __ er

13.  go __ __ les

14.  baseba __ __

15.  ki __ __ ens

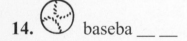

Notes for Home: Your child reviewed words with double consonants in the middle and at the end of words *(happy, shell)*. ***Home Activity:*** Challenge your child to hunt through books for words with double letters. Help your child practice saying and spelling them.

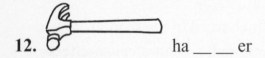

Name ______________________________

Phonics: Long *a*; Long *i*; Long *o* — REVIEW

Directions: Read each sentence. Say the underlined word in each sentence. Choose the word that has the same vowel sound as the underlined word. Mark the space for the answer you have chosen.

1. It was a very nice day.
- ⬭ with
- ⬭ little
- ⬭ dime
- ⬭ dim

2. The sun shone down on the river.
- ⬭ rod
- ⬭ rode
- ⬭ roof
- ⬭ rice

3. The river was not very wide.
- ⬭ gift
- ⬭ which
- ⬭ is
- ⬭ kite

4. It was a good place for the otters.
- ⬭ snake
- ⬭ snap
- ⬭ slice
- ⬭ small

5. Their home was under the bank.
- ⬭ could
- ⬭ cuff
- ⬭ cone
- ⬭ cost

6. Otto and Olga play together.
- ⬭ rattle
- ⬭ sandy
- ⬭ ask
- ⬭ tame

7. She hides on the bank above him.
- ⬭ first
- ⬭ bring
- ⬭ this
- ⬭ fine

8. Then she rolls down the bank.
- ⬭ body
- ⬭ work
- ⬭ spoke
- ⬭ to

9. They both slide into the water.
- ⬭ will
- ⬭ did
- ⬭ dine
- ⬭ winter

10. It's a game they both like.
- ⬭ many
- ⬭ skate
- ⬭ chats
- ⬭ catch

Notes for Home: Your child reviewed words with the long vowel sounds that follow the pattern consonant-vowel-consonant-*e* as in *cake, kite,* and *note.* ***Home Activity:*** Help your child use words like these to write a tale about some mice whose home is a cage.

Name ______________________________

Manual

A **manual** contains directions that help readers use or understand something.

Directions: Use the bicycle manual page to answer the questions.

Different Parts of a Bicycle

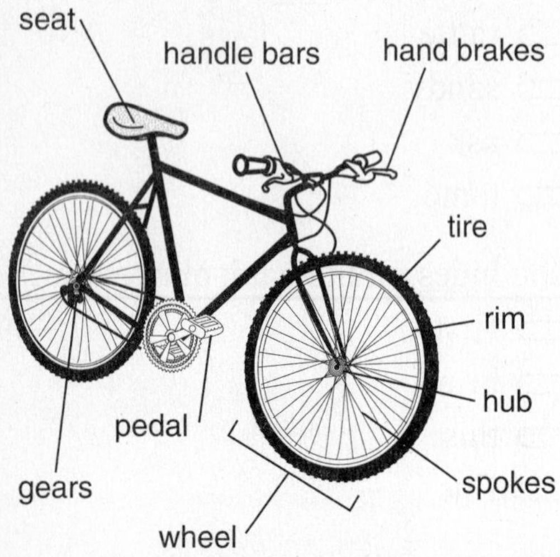

Adjusting the Height of the Seat

Use a wrench to loosen the bolt on the bar beneath the bicycle seat. Raise or lower the seat as needed. Tighten the bolt to hold the seat in place.

Filling a Tire with Air

Locate the nozzle on the inside rim of the tire. Remove the cap from the nozzle. Attach a standard bicycle pump to the nozzle. Use the pump as directed. Fill the tire until it is firm. Remove the pump. Replace the cap and screw it tightly in place.

1. On which part of a bicycle are the spokes? ______________________

2. If you were looking for a good place to ride your bicycle, would you look in a bicycle manual? Explain.

____

____

3. If you needed to replace a pedal, would you look in a bicycle manual? Explain.

____

____

4. What tool would you use to loosen a bolt on a bicycle? ______________________

5. What tool would you use to fill a tire with air? ______________________

Notes for Home: Your child identified the kind of information that is found in a manual. ***Home Activity:*** Show your child a manual that you use such as a home-improvement manual or a car manual. Work together to identify the different kinds of information it contains.

Name ______________________________

Author's Purpose

- **Author's purpose** is the author's reason for writing.
- An author may try to inform, or explain something, or try to entertain you.

Directions: Reread "A Cowboy's Rope." Then complete the web. Tell what you learned about the rope that cowboys use. Then write what you think the author's purpose is and why.

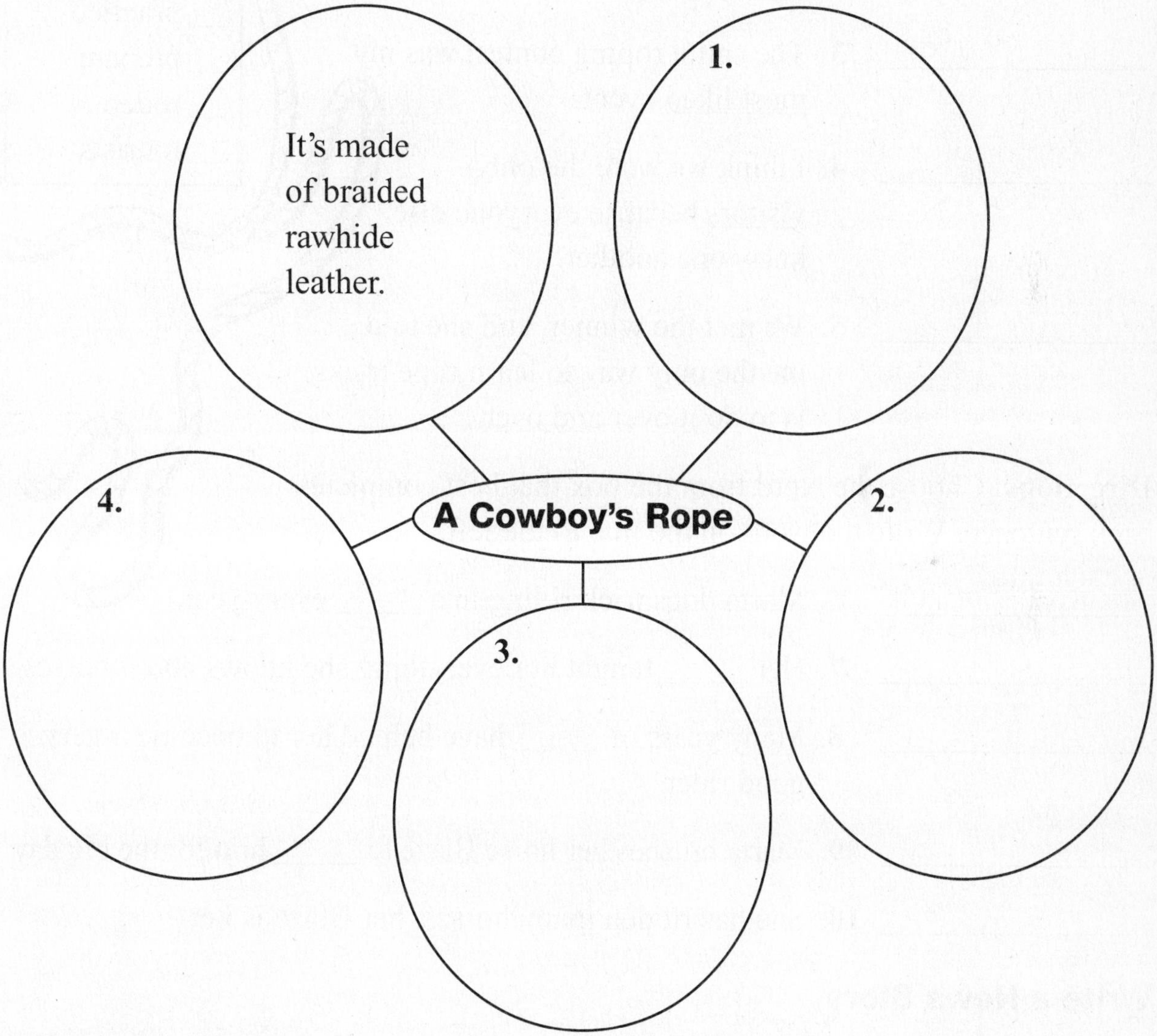
It's made of braided rawhide leather.
1.
A Cowboy's Rope
2.
3.
4.

5. Author's Purpose: ______________________________

____

Notes for Home: Your child used details from the text to figure out an author's reason for writing it. ***Home Activity:*** As you spend time with your child, point out different kinds of texts—ads, comics, newspapers—and ask why an author might have written each kind.

Vocabulary

Directions: Choose the word from the box that best replaces the underlined word or words. Write the word on the line to the left.

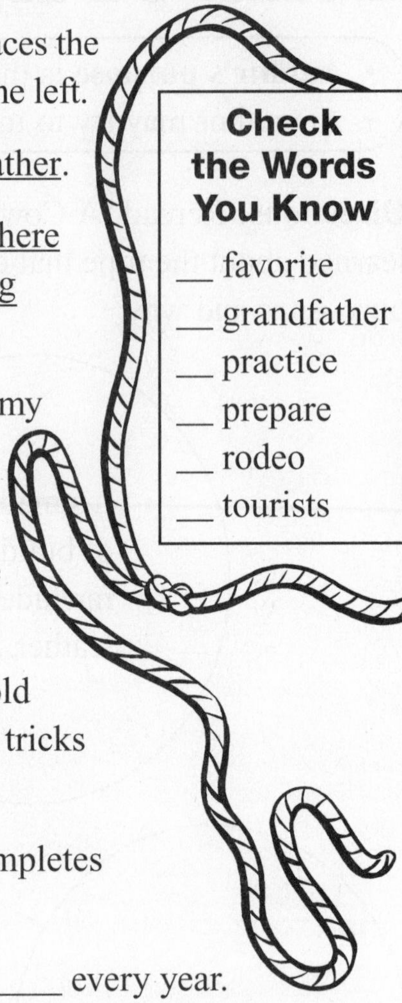

Check the Words You Know

__ favorite
__ grandfather
__ practice
__ prepare
__ rodeo
__ tourists

______________ **1.** We went to visit my <u>father's father</u>.

______________ **2.** He took us to watch a <u>show where people compete in horse riding events</u>.

______________ **3.** The cattle roping contest was my <u>most liked</u> event.

______________ **4.** I think we were the only <u>visitors</u> because everyone else knew one another.

______________ **5.** We met the winner, and she told me the only way to learn rope tricks is to <u>do it over and over</u>.

Directions: Choose the word from the box that best completes each sentence. Write the word on the line to the left.

______________ **6.** Marta does trick riding in a _____ every year.

______________ **7.** Her _____ taught her everything she knows about horses.

______________ **8.** Many years of _____ have helped her to become a very good rider.

______________ **9.** Marta brushes her horse Blaze to _____ him for the big day.

______________ **10.** She has ridden many horses, but Blaze is her _____.

Write a News Story

On a separate sheet of paper, write a news story about a rodeo you just saw. Use as many of the vocabulary words as you can.

Notes for Home: Your child identified and used vocabulary words from *Anthony Reynoso: Born to Rope.* ***Home Activity:*** Ask your child to explain to you what a rodeo is and what happens there. Encourage your child to use as many vocabulary words as possible.

Name ________________________________

Author's Purpose

- **Author's purpose** is the author's reason for writing.
- An author may try to inform, or explain something, or try to entertain you.

Directions: Reread what Anthony tells about his life in *Anthony Reynoso: Born to Rope.* Then answer the questions below.

In Mexico, the Rodeo is the national sport. The most famous charros there are like sports stars here.

On weekdays, Dad runs his landscape business, Mom works in a public school, and I go to school. I wait for the bus with other kids at the corner of my block.

I always come to school with my homework done. When I'm in class, I forget about roping and riding. I don't think anyone in school knows about it except my best friends.

It's different when I get home. I practice hard with Dad. He's a good teacher and shows me everything his father taught him. We spend a lot of time practicing for shows at schools, malls, and rodeos. We are experts at passing the rope. Our next big exhibition is in Sedona, about two hours away by car.

1. Why do you think the authors explain that Rodeo is Mexico's national sport?

____

2. What do the authors want readers to know about Anthony's work as a student?

____

3. Why do you think readers are told that only Anthony's best friends know about his trick roping?

____

4. What message do you think the authors are giving readers by describing the amount of time Anthony spends practicing?

____

5. On a separate sheet of paper, tell why you think the authors wrote about Anthony Reynoso.

Notes for Home: Your child has read a nonfiction text and thought about why the authors chose the information they did. ***Home Activity:*** Read a story with your child. Pause now and then to discuss how the author might want you to think or feel about the characters.

Test-Taking Tips

1. Write your name on the test.
2. Read the directions carefully. Make sure you know exactly what you are supposed to do.
3. Read the question twice. Make sure you understand what the question is asking.
4. Read the answer choices for the question. Eliminate choices that do not make sense.
5. Mark your answer carefully.
6. Check your answer. Make sure that it makes the most sense out of all the answer choices.
7. If you have difficulty answering a question, you may want to go on to the next question. You can come back to difficult questions later.
8. If you finish the test early, go back and check all your answers.

Name ______________________________

Selection Test

Directions: Choose the best answer to each item. Mark the space for the answer you have chosen.

Part 1: Vocabulary

Find the answer choice that means about the same as the underlined word in each sentence.

1. This is my <u>favorite</u> hat.
- ⬭ wide and tall
- ⬭ belonging to a cowboy
- ⬭ liked better than any other
- ⬭ used in a dance

2. Is that your <u>grandfather</u>?
- ⬭ parent of one's father or mother
- ⬭ Mexican cowboy
- ⬭ one who is good with a rope
- ⬭ person who rides horses

3. Did you <u>practice</u> today?
- ⬭ play music
- ⬭ go home after school
- ⬭ feel happy
- ⬭ do many times to get better

4. Several <u>tourists</u> asked me where I live.
- ⬭ people who travel for fun
- ⬭ those who work in a bank
- ⬭ people who ride horses
- ⬭ those who go to school

5. She will <u>prepare</u> lunch.
- ⬭ eat quickly
- ⬭ pay for
- ⬭ make ready
- ⬭ put away

6. We went to the <u>rodeo</u>.
- ⬭ place with many stores
- ⬭ contest of roping and riding
- ⬭ place for looking at art
- ⬭ game played in the water

Part 2: Comprehension

Use what you know about the selection to answer each item.

7. Who seems to be telling this story?
- ⬭ Anthony's mother
- ⬭ Anthony's father
- ⬭ Grandfather Reynoso
- ⬭ Anthony

8. Anthony and his father both like to—
- ⬭ make pictures on rocks.
- ⬭ dance like the Yaqui Indians.
- ⬭ do tricks with a rope.
- ⬭ collect basketball cards.

GO ON

9. What do Anthony and his cousins do on birthdays?
- take a family photo
- go to Casa Reynoso
- have a piñata
- learn to ride horses

10. Anthony can hardly wait to—
- become a basketball player.
- have a baby brother or sister.
- make his own rock carvings.
- swim at Slide Rock.

11. The Yaqui Indian dancers—
- dance every day.
- dance on special holidays.
- ask to have their pictures painted.
- are good friends of the Reynosos.

12. What can Anthony do that his father cannot do?
- play music
- spin a rope with his teeth
- ride a horse
- shoot a basketball

13. The author wrote this selection to—
- tell about Anthony's life.
- teach readers how to rope.
- describe Mexican food.
- tell about the Yaqui Indians.

14. What is Anthony most curious about?
- how Slide Rock came to be
- where his mother works
- how his father learned to rope
- what the rock carvings mean

15. For Anthony's father, it is probably most important for Anthony to—
- carry on the family skill in roping.
- collect as many basketball cards as he can.
- make a lot of money when he grows up.
- keep the secret of the rock carvings in Guadalupe.

STOP

Name ____

REVIEW

Main Idea and Supporting Details

Directions: Read the passage. Then read each question about the passage. Choose the best answer to the question. Mark the space for the answer you have chosen.

Horses Come to America

Horses didn't always exist in North America. The first ones came here with Columbus. The next ones came later with the Spanish pioneers.

The Spanish settlers took horses wherever they went. Spanish pioneers and their horses settled in Mexico and parts of the United States.

The Native Americans of the plains were excited when they saw horses for the first time. They had no big, tame animals that they could ride. They had only dogs to pull loads for them. They saw that horses could change their lives. Horses soon became an important part of their lives.

Some horses broke free of their Spanish owners and ran off. They hid in the hills. These Spanish horses of long ago were the first of the wild mustangs that roam the range even today.

1. This passage tells about—
- ⬭ wild horses.
- ⬭ Spanish pioneers.
- ⬭ Native Americans
- ⬭ how horses came to North America.

2. The first paragraph's main idea is —
- ⬭ that horses didn't always exist in North America.
- ⬭ that the Spanish brought the first horses to America.
- ⬭ that Columbus brought horses with him.
- ⬭ pioneers came from Spain.

3. The second paragraph's main idea is that Spanish pioneers—
- ⬭ built towns and forts.
- ⬭ settled in Mexico.
- ⬭ loved to ride.
- ⬭ took horses into new areas.

4. The third paragraph's main idea is that Native Americans—
- ⬭ quickly wanted and used horses.
- ⬭ were very good riders.
- ⬭ used dogs to pull loads.
- ⬭ were surprised to see horses.

5. The last paragraph's main idea is that Spanish horses—
- ⬭ didn't like their owners.
- ⬭ liked to hide in the hills.
- ⬭ are ancestors of wild mustangs.
- ⬭ lived long ago.

Notes for Home: Your child identified the main ideas of a passage and its paragraphs. ***Home Activity:*** As you read nonfiction material with your child, pause occasionally to ask your child to tell you the main idea of a specific paragraph or section.

Name ________________________________

Phonics: Long e Digraphs; Long e Spelled *y* and e

Directions: Choose the word with the **long e** sound to complete each sentence. Write the word on the line.

________________ **1.** Yesterday I had a (birthday/party).

________________ **2.** I wore my new (jeans/sweater).

________________ **3.** My brother hung a piñata, a paper animal filled with fun things, on our (deck/tree).

________________ **4.** It looked like a red and (green/yellow) bird.

________________ **5.** We spread a (blanket/sheet) on the ground below.

________________ **6.** (Candy/Gum) fell out of it when it was broken.

________________ **7.** Then everyone had a big (slice/piece) of cake.

________________ **8.** I felt really (great/happy)!

Directions: Circle the word with the **long e** sound. Then underline the letter or letters that stand for that vowel sound.

9. been	feel	fell
10. learn	teacher	test
11. busy	cry	played
12. felt	flies	field
13. we	were	wet
14. friend	guess	shield
15. teeth	tents	try

Notes for Home: Your child reviewed words in which the long *e* sound is spelled *e, ie, ee, ea,* or *y*. ***Home Activity:*** Have your child make a collage of magazine pictures showing items that have a long *e* sound in their names. Help your child label each item with its name.

Name ____

Phonics: Double Consonants

REVIEW

Directions: Read each sentence. Find the word that makes sense in each sentence. Mark the space for the answer you have chosen.

1. The rabbits ___ on the lettuce.
- nibble
- nimble
- napped
- nodded

2. I lost a wool ___.
- mitten
- mission
- middle
- muddle

3. I have plans for my ___ vacation.
- slipper
- supper
- sudden
- summer

4. Sweep up that ___ on the floor.
- still
- stuff
- sell
- stall

5. I have only a ___ popcorn left.
- jolly
- litter
- little
- ladder

6. They ___ apples for ten cents each.
- silly
- seal
- sell
- self

7. The fire ___ rang.
- belt
- bell
- bellow
- bugle

8. I like jam on my ___.
- muffin
- mitten
- middle
- muffler

9. We eat ___ at six o'clock.
- dinner
- dimmer
- super
- diner

10. The boy ___ softly on the window.
- tall
- taped
- toss
- tapped

Notes for Home: Your child reviewed words with double consonants found in the middle or at the end *(summer, spill)*. ***Home Activity:*** Have your child look through the television listings for words with double consonants and circle them. Encourage him or her to read the words aloud.

Name ______________________________

Maps

Maps are drawings of places that can show you cities, states, and countries. They can also show roads, hills, mountains, and bodies of water.

Directions: Study the map of Felicia's family trip. Then answer the questions.

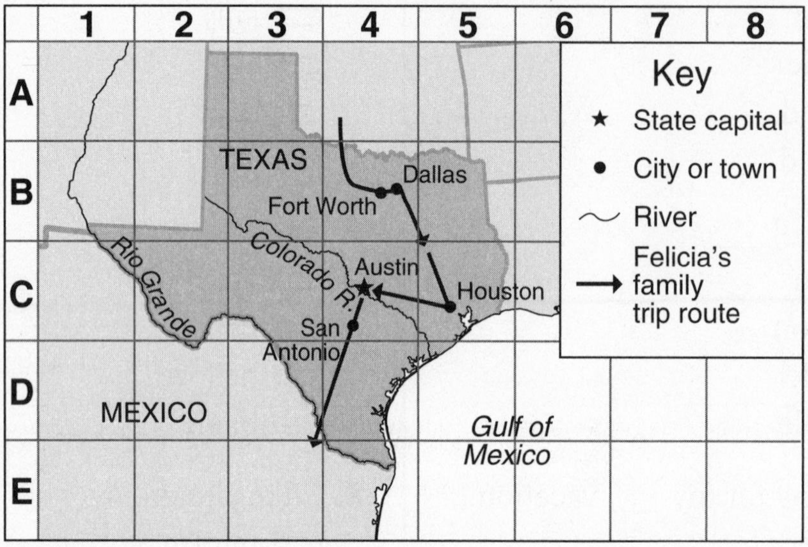

1. What is the state capital of Texas? ______________________

2. After visiting the state capital, which city did Felicia's family visit next? How do you know?

____

____

3. What number and letter tell the location of Fort Worth? What city is located in the area 5-C?

____

4. What large body of water borders Texas? ______________________

5. If you wanted to know how to find a specific street in Houston, would you look at a map of the city of Houston or the state of Texas? Explain.

____

____

Notes for Home: Your child read a map and answered questions about it. ***Home Activity:*** Look at a map of your state or city with your child. Mark a route you have taken or plan to take. Talk about different places or landmarks and where they are in relation to each other.

Cause and Effect

- A **cause** is why something happens. An **effect** is what happens.
- Clue words can sometimes signal causes and effects.
- As you read, look for clue words, such as *if, then, because, since,* and *so,* to help you understand what happens and why it happens.

Cause → Effect

Directions: Reread "Annabelle's Party." Then complete the diagram. Write a cause for each effect given.

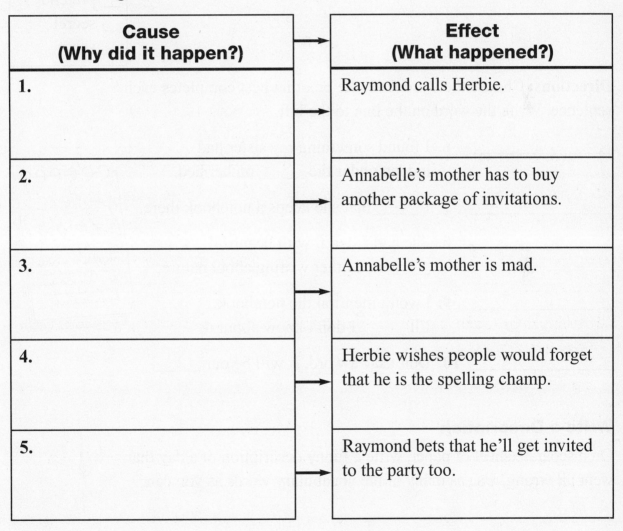

Cause (Why did it happen?)		Effect (What happened?)
1.	→	Raymond calls Herbie.
2.	→	Annabelle's mother has to buy another package of invitations.
3.	→	Annabelle's mother is mad.
4.	→	Herbie wishes people would forget that he is the spelling champ.
5.	→	Raymond bets that he'll get invited to the party too.

Notes for Home: Your child read a story and explained the causes of story events. ***Home Activity:*** Talk about the weather in your area. Encourage your child to identify some of the effects the weather has had on your daily life, such as having to use an umbrella.

Name ____________________

Vocabulary

Directions: Draw a line to match each word with its definition.

1. sheet	make believe
2. coughs	eager to know
3. pretend	found out
4. discovered	a piece of cloth on a bed
5. curious	forces out air from lungs repeatedly with sudden noises

Check the Words You Know

__ coughs
__ curious
__ discovered
__ poems
__ pretend
__ secret
__ sheet

Directions: Choose the word from the box that best completes each sentence. Write the word on the line to the left.

________________ **6.** I found something my sister had hidden under the _____ on her bed.

________________ **7.** I _____ that she keeps a notebook there.

________________ **8.** She had filled it with beautiful _____ and other writing about nature.

________________ **9.** I won't mention the notebook. I'll _____ I don't know about it.

________________ **10.** Don't say a word. It will be our _____.

Write a Description

On a separate sheet of paper, write a funny description of a day that went all wrong. Use as many of the vocabulary words as you can.

Notes for Home: Your child identified and used vocabulary words from *Herbie and Annabelle. **Home Activity:*** Help your child write a poem about being sick. Use as many vocabulary words as possible. *(I had the day off because I had a cough!)*

Cause and Effect

- A **cause** is why something happens. An **effect** is what happens.
- As you read, look for clue words, such as *if, then, because, since,* and *so,* to help you understand what happens and why it happens.

Directions: Reread what happens in *Herbie and Annabelle* when Herbie arrives at Annabelle's house. Then answer the questions below.

HERBIE: I wish I didn't have to deliver these get well cards from the class. But the teacher said I *had* to because I live the closest. *(groans)*
NARRATOR: Mr. Hodgekiss answered the door.
MR. HODGEKISS: Hello, Herbie.
HERBIE: Hello, Mr. Hodgekiss. My teacher wanted me to drop these cards by for Annabelle. Would you please give them to her? *(waves good-bye)* Thanks, bye.
NARRATOR: Herbie turned around and headed down the steps.
MR. HODGEKISS: Just a minute, Herbie. Won't you come in and give the cards to Annabelle yourself? The doctor says she isn't contagious anymore. . . .
NARRATOR: Herbie felt his throat getting dry and raspy as he walked inside the house. When they got to Annabelle's door, they stopped.

1. Why is Herbie asked to deliver the get well cards to Annabelle?

____

2. Why does Herbie quickly turn around and start to go back down the steps?

____

3. What makes Herbie go inside to see Annabelle? ______________________________

____

4. Why does Herbie's throat get dry and raspy? ______________________________

____

5. On a separate sheet of paper, tell why you think Herbie did not want to talk to Annabelle.

Notes for Home: Your child read dialogue and explained the causes and effects of events. ***Home Activity:*** Make up if/then statements with your child. One person uses *if* to describe something that could happen, while the other person uses *then* to describe a possible effect.

Test-Taking Tips

1. Write your name on the test.
2. Read the directions carefully. Make sure you know exactly what you are supposed to do.
3. Read the question twice. Make sure you understand what the question is asking.
4. Read the answer choices for the question. Eliminate choices that do not make sense.
5. Mark your answer carefully.
6. Check your answer. Make sure that it makes the most sense out of all the answer choices.
7. If you have difficulty answering a question, you may want to go on to the next question. You can come back to difficult questions later.
8. If you finish the test early, go back and check all your answers.

Name ____________________

Selection Test

Directions: Choose the best answer to each item. Mark the space for the answer you have chosen.

Part 1: Vocabulary

Find the answer choice that means about the same as the underlined word in each sentence.

1. My teddy bear is under the sheet.
- top of a house
- pile of books
- covering on a bed
- rug used to cover a floor

2. Dad sometimes coughs in the morning.
- forces air from the lungs in a noisy way
- draws a picture
- laughs in a way that cannot be heard
- speaks loudly

3. Dick's lie was discovered quickly.
- told again
- covered up
- written well
- found out

4. Mary will pretend to be sick.
- try hard
- make believe
- forget how
- remember

5. Sherry likes those poems.
- picture books
- people who dance well
- happy songs
- pieces of writing with rhymes

6. His real name is a secret.
- something kept hidden
- funny word
- something hard to read
- good joke

7. I'm curious about what is in this box.
- bored
- eager to know
- greedy
- heavy

Part 2: Comprehension

Use what you know about the play to answer each item.

8. Herbie went to Annabelle's house to—
- make fun of her.
- give her some cards.
- ask why she was not in school.
- help with her homework.

GO ON

9. Herbie was picked to go to Annabelle's because—

- ⬭ he lived closest to her.
- ⬭ he knew her best.
- ⬭ he made the best card.
- ⬭ he knew Mr. Hodgekiss.

10. When Herbie visited, Mr. Hodgekiss hoped that Annabelle would—

- ⬭ take the sheet off her head.
- ⬭ get over the chicken pox.
- ⬭ give the chicken pox to Herbie.
- ⬭ tell Herbie how she felt.

11. What did Annabelle put in her notepad beside Herbie's name?

- ⬭ three stars
- ⬭ a red rose
- ⬭ a Viking ship
- ⬭ three red checks

12. The only thing Annabelle said she liked about Herbie was that he—

- ⬭ gave her a can of salmon.
- ⬭ looked like a pirate.
- ⬭ had a way with words.
- ⬭ wrote a story about her.

13. Annabelle thought Raymond Martin's card was dumb because it—

- ⬭ had a picture on it.
- ⬭ said "Bon Voyage."
- ⬭ had a poem in it.
- ⬭ said "don't get well."

14. What did Herbie do at the end to make himself sound like John Greenweed?

- ⬭ held a Kleenex over his mouth
- ⬭ spoke in a soft whisper
- ⬭ held up two fingers for victory
- ⬭ made up a poem

15. What can you tell about Herbie and Annabelle from this play?

- ⬭ They both like to eat salmon.
- ⬭ They both like to wear costumes.
- ⬭ They pretend they don't like each other, but they do.
- ⬭ They try to be nice to each other, but they don't get along.

STOP

Drawing Conclusions

REVIEW

Directions: Read the story. Then read each question about the story. Choose the best answer to the question. Mark the space for the answer you have chosen.

A Special Kind of Chicken Pox

Tony's mom stood in the doorway, pulling on her coat. She had a worried look on her face.

"Don't be late for your meeting, Amy," said Grandma. "I'll take good care of Tony."

Tony was glad to hear the door bang shut behind his mother. Now all he had to do was keep his grandmother from coming too close. He wasn't sure how real the pink marks on his face looked.

"Better stay away, Grandma," he said. "You might catch it."

"Don't worry, Tony," said Grandma. "I've already had that kind of chicken pox before. I still get it now and then." She grinned and left the room.

1. Tony's mother—
- has just come indoors.
- is worried about leaving Tony.
- is going to find a doctor.
- doesn't think Tony is sick.

2. Grandma is visiting because she—
- has a meeting.
- can't catch chicken pox.
- will take care of Tony.
- came to see Tony's mom.

3. Tony doesn't want Grandma to—
- stay in the house.
- leave the room.
- catch chicken pox from him.
- find out that his chicken pox is not real.

4. Grandma lets Tony know that—
- she's good at taking care of sick people.
- she knows he isn't really sick.
- she's afraid of catching his chicken pox.
- she gets sick often.

5. Grandma's grin shows that—
- she's not mad at Tony for pretending to be sick.
- she's going to tell his mother.
- Tony looks really funny.
- she isn't feeling well either.

Notes for Home: Your child has read a passage and used details in it to draw conclusions. ***Home Activity:*** Watch a TV show with your child. During breaks, ask your child to draw conclusions about the characters' feelings or why they act the way they do.

Name ______________________________

Phonics: Long *a* Digraphs; Long *o* Digraphs; Long *o* Spelled *o*

Directions: Choose the word with the **long a** or **long o** sound that best matches each definition. Write the word on the line.

________	**1.** all right	glad	okay	well
________	**2.** a sound that expresses pain	groan	growl	sob
________	**3.** something that can carry water	can	jar	pail
________	**4.** coverings for the body	dresses	cloth	clothes
________	**5.** heat until brown	cook	toast	broil
________	**6.** made something fall into pieces	broke	chopped	cracked

Directions: Circle the word that has the **long a** or **long o** sound. Then underline the letter or letters in the word that stand for that vowel sound.

7. got	who	go
8. dance	play	watch
9. sail	salt	slam
10. gorilla	good	gold
11. last	laps	layer
12. raise	rabbit	bread
13. moss	most	mess
14. through	throat	thought
15. stand	start	stay

Notes for Home: Your child reviewed words in which long *a* is spelled *ay* and *ai* and words in which long *o* is spelled *o* and *oa*. ***Home Activity:*** Take turns writing movie, song, TV, or book titles with long *a (play)* or long *o* words *(go)* in them (for example: *Home Alone*).

Name ______________________________

REVIEW

Phonics: Long e Digraphs; Long e: *y*, e

Directions: Read each sentence. Choose the word that has the **long e** sound heard in **see** to complete each sentence. Mark the space for the answer you have chosen.

1. Jan needs to ___ after lunch.
- play
- rest
- sleep
- dress

2. It isn't ___ to stay in bed and do nothing.
- time
- okay
- best
- easy

3. She got ___ cards from friends.
- seven
- many
- eight
- less

4. She has been reading ___ books.
- new
- old
- these
- her

5. The card from her ___ makes her smile.
- teacher
- neighbor
- dentist
- friends

6. She tried to ___ out of bed this morning.
- stay
- get
- step
- creep

7. She was so ___ that she had to get back in bed.
- weak
- rested
- tired
- bored

8. She still feels a little ___.
- shy
- dizzy
- better
- excited

9. Her mother gave her some ___ soup.
- fresh
- vegetable
- bean
- chicken

10. ___ will feel better soon.
- She
- Mother
- Her
- Jan

Notes for Home: Your child reviewed words with the long *e* sound spelled *e, ee, ea,* and *y* (*he, see, beach, funny*). ***Home Activity:*** Help your child write sentences that use long *e* words. Have your child circle the letters that represent the long *e* sound.

Name ____________________

Technology: Locate/Collect Information

Directions: Find titles of audiotapes, films, and videotapes available in a library media center. Then answer the questions.

Audiotapes 

Jump, Skip, Run: Exercises for Young People
Songs and Games
Music for Ballet
Move with Us

Films 

The Game of Soccer
Ten Ways to Stay Fit
Math Is Fun
Learn to Make Puppets

Videotapes 

Staying Fit
Eating Well
Healthy Food
Swimming

1. What kind of media could you use if you were interested in learning about healthy snacks?

____

2. If your teacher suggested you watch two films on exercise, which ones would you watch?

____

3. In which section of the library media center would you look if you needed music to play for a class performance—audiotapes, films, or videos?

____

4. What kind of media could you use to learn about making puppets?

____

5. If you wanted to use an exercise tape, would you choose an audiotape or a videotape? Explain.

____

____

Notes for Home: Your child answered questions about different kinds of media found in a library. ***Home Activity:*** Visit the library with your child. Point out different sections of the library media center. Discuss with your child the kinds of information available within the media center.

Name ____________________

Character

- A **character** is a person or animal in a story.
- Authors tell us about characters when they describe what characters say, do, and feel.

Directions: Reread "The Newcomer." Then complete the table. Read what the characters say or do. Write a sentence that tells what this shows about each character.

Character	Action or Words	What This Shows
Aunt Laura	She was the first to say yes to taking Kevin.	**1.**
	"We're delighted to have you come stay with us."	**2.**
Kevin	He came without any clothes, toys, or parents.	**3.**
Dawn	"How come that raggedy little boy has to come live with us?"	**4.**
	She hangs up a sign that says: NO LITTLE BOYS ALLOWED.	**5.**

Notes for Home: Your child has read a story and looked at characters' words and actions to learn more about them. ***Home Activity:*** Invite your child to describe her or his friends. Discuss how the things they say and do show what they are like.

Vocabulary

Directions: Write about an exciting moment in a game. Use the five vocabulary words below.

aimed
basketball
bounced
playground
shoot

Check the Words You Know

__ aimed
__ basketball
__ bounced
__ gift
__ playground
__ shoot

1.–5. ______________________________

____

____

____

____

Directions: Circle **T** if the sentence is true. Circle **F** if it is false.

6. A basketball is the size of a child's fist. T F

7. There may be slides and swings on a playground. T F

8. You should always return a gift as soon as you are done with it. T F

9. In baseball you try to hit a ball, and in basketball you try to shoot a basket. T F

10. If you made a free throw shot, you probably aimed carefully. T F

Write Advice

On a separate sheet of paper, list some good advice for new basketball players. Use as many of the vocabulary words as you can.

Notes for Home: Your child identified and used vocabulary words from *Allie's Basketball Dream*. ***Home Activity:*** Invite your child to pretend he or she is a sportscaster. Your child can give you a "live" report, using the vocabulary words.

Name ______________________________

Character

- A **character** is a person or animal in a story.
- Authors tell us about characters when they describe what characters say, do, and feel.

Directions: Reread what happens in *Allie's Basketball Dream* when Allie practices with her new basketball. Then answer the questions below.

"Go ahead and practice, and then we'll shoot baskets together as soon as I get back from taking Aunt Harriet shopping," Allie's father told her. "I'll just be across the street. If you need me, tell Mr. Gonzalez, and he'll come get me."

"Okay," Allie replied.

She waved good-bye and ran to an empty court. She lifted her new basketball over her head and aimed. The shot missed. She aimed again. She missed again.

One of the boys playing in the next court noticed Allie and started to laugh. The others joined in.

"*Boys,*" Allie mumbled. Then she dribbled and bounced. And bounced and dribbled.

1. What do you think Allie's father's words to Allie show about him?

____

2. What does Allie's reply to her father show about Allie? ______________________________

____

3. What do you learn about the boys based on the way they act? ______________________________

____

____

4. What does Allie's reaction to the boys show about Allie? ______________________________

____

5. On a separate sheet of paper, tell what you learn about Allie from what she says, does, and feels. Give an example from the story.

Notes for Home: Your child read about what some characters said and did and used this information to tell what the characters are like. ***Home Activity:*** Have your child tell you about his or her favorite story character and how he or she could tell what the character was like.

Test-Taking Tips

1. Write your name on the test.
2. Read the directions carefully. Make sure you know exactly what you are supposed to do.
3. Read the question twice. Make sure you understand what the question is asking.
4. Read the answer choices for the question. Eliminate choices that do not make sense.
5. Mark your answer carefully.
6. Check your answer. Make sure that it makes the most sense out of all the answer choices.
7. If you have difficulty answering a question, you may want to go on to the next question. You can come back to difficult questions later.
8. If you finish the test early, go back and check all your answers.

Name ______________________________________

Selection Test

Directions: Choose the best answer to each item. Mark the space for the answer you have chosen.

Part 1: Vocabulary

Find the answer choice that means about the same as the underlined word in each sentence.

1. I got a <u>gift</u> from my mom.
- ⬭ ride in a car
- ⬭ present
- ⬭ kiss on the nose
- ⬭ hug

2. Gail got ready to <u>shoot</u>.
- ⬭ send a ball toward the goal
- ⬭ pass a ball to someone
- ⬭ catch a ball
- ⬭ put air into a ball

3. Mike <u>aimed</u> the water gun.
- ⬭ filled with water
- ⬭ shot
- ⬭ lost
- ⬭ pointed at a target

4. Denny <u>bounced</u> the ball.
- ⬭ threw it hard
- ⬭ held onto it
- ⬭ caused it to spring back
- ⬭ took it away

5. We went to the <u>playground</u>.
- ⬭ a tall building
- ⬭ a large hall where shows are held
- ⬭ a place for outdoor play
- ⬭ a box filled with sand

6. Do you have a <u>basketball</u>?
- ⬭ ring with a net
- ⬭ ball used in a game
- ⬭ place where a game is played
- ⬭ ball made to be kicked

Part 2: Comprehension

Use what you know about the story to answer each item.

7. Allie got a basketball from—
- ⬭ Mr. Puchinsky.
- ⬭ her friend Sheba.
- ⬭ Mr. Gonzalez.
- ⬭ her father.

8. In this story, Domino is a—
- ⬭ basketball player.
- ⬭ dog.
- ⬭ friend of Allie's.
- ⬭ fire captain.

GO ON

9. When Allie saw some older boys playing nearby, she felt a little—
   - sad.
   - pleased.
   - angry.
   - nervous.

10. Keisha did not want to play basketball because she thought—
    - basketball was a boys' game.
    - Allie should try jumping rope.
    - volleyball was the best game.
    - Allie should do her homework.

11. Which sentence best tells what kind of person Allie is?
    - She has trouble making friends.
    - She likes to sit around the house.
    - She tells everyone what to do.
    - She tries hard and does not give up.

12. The boys in the next court laughed at Allie because she—
    - could not lift the ball.
    - threw the ball in a trash can.
    - kept missing the basket.
    - used her ball to play soccer.

13. Which thing happened before Allie got the new basketball?
    - She got some gum from Buddy.
    - She went to a game at Madison Square Garden.
    - She went to the playground.
    - She played with a hula hoop.

14. By the end of the story, Buddy was the one who—
    - believed most in Allie's dream.
    - played basketball best.
    - told Allie to forget her dream.
    - laughed loudest at Allie.

15. Which of these could **not** really happen?
    - Allie blows purple bubbles.
    - The ball goes in the basket without touching the backboard.
    - Allie throws the ball into a trash can.
    - Domino plays basketball.

STOP

Cause and Effect

REVIEW

Directions: Read the story. Then read each question about the story. Choose the best answer to the question. Mark the space for the answer you have chosen.

A Skinned Knee and Good Friends

Kendra hit the volleyball over the net. Two players on the other side both ran forward. Ryan fell against Jackie, and she fell to the ground.

"I'm sorry," said Ryan.

Kendra and her teammate Logan ran to help. Jackie's knee was bleeding. Ryan helped Jackie hop to a bench, while Logan ran for a wet paper towel. Just then a car honked outside the playground.

Ryan turned to look. "That's Mom," he told Logan.

"Come on," said Logan to Jackie. "She'll give you a ride home."

The boys helped Jackie hop to their mother's car. Kendra watched them go. She bounced the ball a few times. Then she started for home too.

1. What made Ryan say he was sorry?
- He missed the ball.
- He hit Jackie with the ball.
- He hit Kendra with the ball.
- He made Jackie fall.

2. What happened because of Jackie's fall?
- They agreed to end their game.
- Jackie hurt her knee.
- Logan called his Mom.
- Ryan fell down too.

3. When the car horn honked, what happened?
- Logan's mother began to wave.
- Jackie asked for a ride home.
- Ryan turned to see who it was.
- Ryan and Logan ran to see who it was.

4. Why did Ryan and Logan leave?
- Their mother came to get them.
- They needed to get Jackie to a doctor.
- Jackie couldn't play anymore.
- Ryan felt bad about bumping into Jackie.

5. Why did Kendra go home?
- Her team had won the game.
- There was no one left to play.
- She was worried about Jackie.
- She had to catch a bus.

Notes for Home: Your child identified causes and effects in a story. ***Home Activity:*** Make up an event for your child to think about. Explore the things that this event would cause to happen. For example: *What would happen if a gorilla walked into your classroom?*

Phonics: Long *i* spelled *igh* and *y*; Long *u* spelled *u-e* and *u*

Directions: Circle the word with the **long i** or the **long u** sound. Then write the word in the puzzle.

Down

1. quit music mouse
2. eight which right
4. really risky reply
6. must sum menu
9. sigh sick silly

Across

3. under unlucky uniform
5. cut cute court
7. type city yet
8. us our use
10. lily light lick

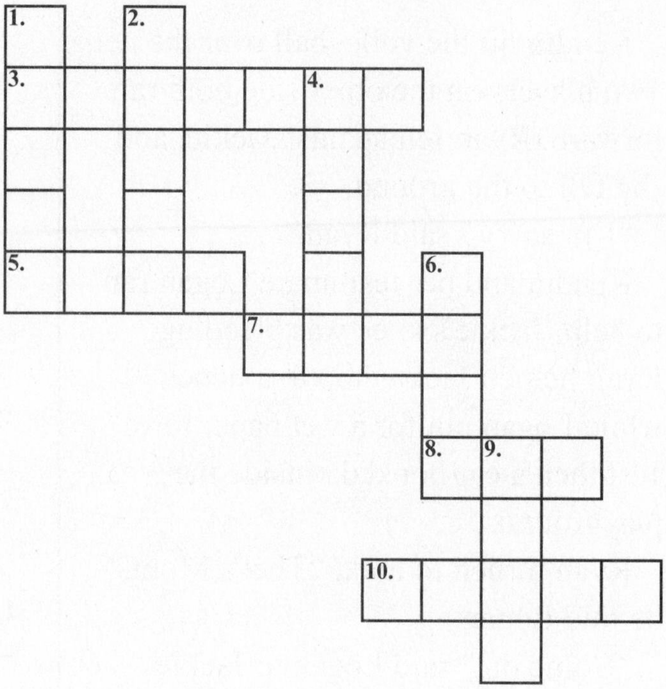

Directions: Choose the word with the **long i** or **long u** sound to complete each sentence. Write the word on the line.

______________ **11.** Our park has a (bumpy/huge) playing field.

______________ **12.** It's the same (size/width) as a big league field.

______________ **13.** (My/This) team is called the Cubs.

______________ **14.** Wow! That ball was really (swift/high)!

______________ **15.** A runner goes (skidding/flying) past third base.

Notes for Home: Your child reviewed words in which the long *i* is spelled *igh (right)* and *y (cry)* and the long *u* is spelled *u-e (use)* and *u (music)*. ***Home Activity:*** Read aloud with your child. Help your child find and say words with the long *i* and long *u* sounds.

Name ______________________________

Phonics: Short Vowels

REVIEW

Directions: Read each sentence. Say the underlined word or syllable in each sentence. Choose the word that has the same vowel sound as the underlined word or syllable. Mark the space for the answer you have chosen.

1. Brenna passed the ball to Kit.
- ⬭ that
- ⬭ talk
- ⬭ chased
- ⬭ tape

2. Teri tried to block the ball.
- ⬭ don't
- ⬭ rodeo
- ⬭ popped
- ⬭ board

3. Kit threw it over Teri's head.
- ⬭ three
- ⬭ mean
- ⬭ west
- ⬭ sad

4. Molly dribbled the ball.
- ⬭ light
- ⬭ their
- ⬭ lift
- ⬭ shined

5. Molly took a shot at the basket.
- ⬭ whole
- ⬭ show
- ⬭ goes
- ⬭ hop

6. The ball thumped against the backboard.
- ⬭ buy
- ⬭ bunk
- ⬭ your
- ⬭ used

7. Molly had missed the basket.
- ⬭ smiled
- ⬭ gift
- ⬭ wild
- ⬭ liked

8. Kit got the ball next.
- ⬭ few
- ⬭ seed
- ⬭ bead
- ⬭ when

9. She carefully aimed at the basket.
- ⬭ trash
- ⬭ aimed
- ⬭ bacon
- ⬭ bake

10. The ball brushed the rim and went in.
- ⬭ just
- ⬭ would
- ⬭ music
- ⬭ four

Notes for Home: Your child reviewed words with short vowel sounds heard in *bat, bed, bit, hot,* and *but*. ***Home Activity:*** Use a newspaper to point out two- and three-syllable words with short vowel sounds such as *basket*. Ask your child to read these words aloud.

Name ______________________________

Magazines/Newsletters

Directions: Read the newsletter. Use it to answer the questions below.

Basketball News

Thompson Brings Victory

Tina Thompson scored 10 points in last night's game leading Gino's Giants to victory over Shawn's Shooting Stars. Both teams came into the game with a 3–0 record. Although the Shooting Stars played well, Thompson was the real shooting star of the evening.

Letters to the Editor

Dear Editor,
I think basketball is the best sport around. Not only is it great exercise, but it is fun too. Basketball players are the greatest athletes in the world.
Bouncing Bob

Advertisements

Old and new basketball cards in mint condition. Buy Now!
Call 55P-LAY-BALL.

1. What is the name of the newsletter? ______________________________

2. Who might subscribe to this newsletter?

____

3. If you wanted to sell a backboard and basketball, how might you use the newsletter?

____

____

4. What is the name of the news story? ______________________________

5. Which section lets readers express their opinions? ______________________________

Notes for Home: Your child read a newsletter and answered questions about it. ***Home Activity:*** Read a simple magazine or newsletter. Have your child point out the different parts. Then challenge your child to write a news story, an advertisement, or an editorial.

Name ______________________________________

Graphic Sources

- A **graphic source** can be a picture, diagram, map, chart, graph, or something else that shows information.
- Graphic sources are useful because they show lots of information in an easy-to-see way.
- Making your own graphic, such as a chart, picture, or diagram, can help you understand what you read.

Directions: Reread "Flowering Plants." Use the words and the picture to help you complete the table. Write the facts that tell about the parts of the flowering plant and how long different kinds can live.

Flowering Plants

Kinds	peas, beans, corn, roses, tomatoes, most trees
Size	Some are so small you can hardly see them.
	Some are the largest living things.
Parts	flower
	seed
	fruit
	1.
	2.
	3.
How Long They Live	Some grow for many years.
	4.
	5.

Notes for Home: Your child used information from a nonfiction passage and a labeled picture to complete a table. ***Home Activity:*** Work with your child to think of ways that a table would help in planning a schedule for afterschool activities.

Name ________________________________

Vocabulary

Directions: Choose the word from the box that best matches each definition. Write the word on the line.

Check the Words You Know

__ collect
__ hinge
__ insects
__ pitcher
__ plants
__ trap

________________ **1.** something that can catch animals

________________ **2.** a container to hold liquids

________________ **3.** something that joins two parts but allows the parts to move

________________ **4.** small animals with bodies that are divided into three parts

________________ **5.** gather together

________________ **6.** living things that can make their own food from light and air

Directions: Choose the word from the box that best completes each sentence. Write the word on the line to the left.

________________ **7.** I like to watch ants and other _____.

________________ **8.** I see them on the _____ my mother grows in the yard.

________________ **9.** Once I tried to catch a ladybug in a _____ .

________________ **10.** I put it in a special box, but the _____ was broken and the lid came off.

Write an Advertisement

Imagine that you own a garden store. On a separate sheet of paper, write an advertisement for your plants. Describe how to take care of them. Use as many of the vocabulary words as you can.

Notes for Home: Your child identified and used vocabulary words from *Fly Traps! Plants That Bite Back*. ***Home Activity:*** With your child, read a book or a magazine article about plants and insects. Encourage your child to look for the vocabulary words while reading.

Name ______________________________

Graphic Sources

- A **graphic source** can be a picture, diagram, map, chart, graph, or something else that shows information.
- Graphic sources are useful because they show lots of information in an easy-to-see way.
- Making your own graphic, such as a chart, picture, or diagram, can help you understand what you read.

Directions: Reread about cobra lilies in *Fly Traps! Plants That Bite Back.* Then answer the questions below.

This one caught insects, too, but it didn't actually do very much. It had leaves like funnels, with a slippery rim and a little pool at the bottom.

When insects crawled inside, they fell into the pool and couldn't climb out. So they stayed there and became bug soup for the lily.

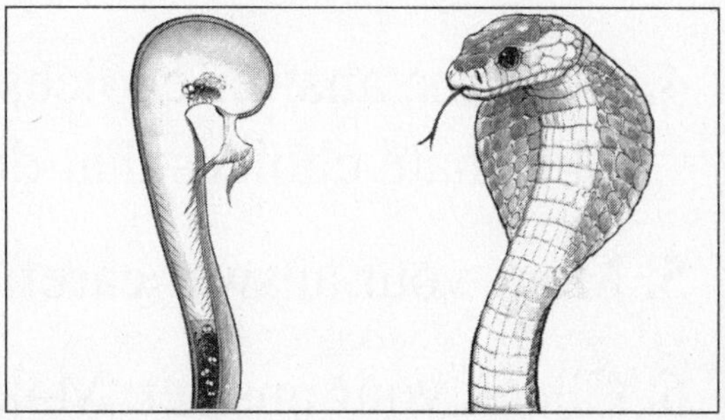

1. Why was the cobra lily given its name?

____

2. Based on the picture and the text, how would you describe a cobra lily's leaf?

____

3. Where do insects get into the leaf?

____

4. Where in the leaf do the insects end up?

____

5. On a separate sheet of paper, draw a picture showing how a sundew eats insects.

Notes for Home: Your child answered questions using information from a nonfiction text and pictures. ***Home Activity:*** Help your child use pictures in a nonfiction book to understand its information better. Ask your child questions based on the pictures.

Name ______________________________

Test-Taking Tips

1. Write your name on the test.
2. Read the directions carefully. Make sure you know exactly what you are supposed to do.
3. Read the question twice. Make sure you understand what the question is asking.
4. Read the answer choices for the question. Eliminate choices that do not make sense.
5. Mark your answer carefully.
6. Check your answer. Make sure that it makes the most sense out of all the answer choices.
7. If you have difficulty answering a question, you may want to go on to the next question. You can come back to difficult questions later.
8. If you finish the test early, go back and check all your answers.

Selection Test

Directions: Choose the best answer to each item. Mark the space for the answer you have chosen.

Part 1: Vocabulary

Find the answer choice that means about the same as the underlined word in each sentence.

1. I found the insects.
- ⬭ leaves from a tree
- ⬭ small blades of grass
- ⬭ sweet, red fruits
- ⬭ small, six-legged animals

2. Carla likes to collect stamps.
- ⬭ give away
- ⬭ put in a safe place
- ⬭ gather together
- ⬭ look closely at

3. Is that hinge broken?
- ⬭ a round handle on a door
- ⬭ a joint between two moving parts
- ⬭ a tool used for cutting
- ⬭ a door in a wall

4. Jessica has lots of plants.
- ⬭ living things that grow in soil
- ⬭ stones or rocks
- ⬭ black and white photos
- ⬭ special books about animals

5. Mrs. Lewis bought a pitcher.
- ⬭ a container for holding liquids
- ⬭ a tool like a large fork
- ⬭ a glove used in baseball
- ⬭ a painting or drawing

6. Felix checked the trap.
- ⬭ a shelter that can be moved
- ⬭ a thing for catching animals
- ⬭ a hanging bed or couch
- ⬭ an outdoor table and chairs

Part 2: Comprehension

Use what you know about the selection to answer each item.

7. What does the narrator like to do?
- ⬭ grow giant leeks
- ⬭ watch plants that eat animals
- ⬭ collect yogurt containers
- ⬭ make models out of bottle tops

8. What does the sundew use to catch bugs?
- ⬭ trap doors
- ⬭ bladders
- ⬭ sharp teeth
- ⬭ sticky leaves

GO ON

9. Plants that eat animals do not like—
   - fertilizer.
   - sunlight.
   - water.
   - insects.

10. Which is the biggest kind of sundew?
   - rainbow sundew
   - African sundew
   - round-leaf sundew
   - English sundew

11. Ants can escape from a Venus flytrap because they—
   - do not taste good.
   - eat through the leaves.
   - cannot be dissolved.
   - are small enough to crawl out.

12. The narrator went to Malaysia to—
   - take a vacation.
   - learn about the people there.
   - visit some friends.
   - look for pitcher plants.

13. How are cobra lilies different from Venus flytraps?
   - They catch bugs.
   - They eat insects.
   - They are bigger.
   - They live in the water.

14. Cobra lilies look like—
   - spiders.
   - African sundews.
   - snakes.
   - bladderworts.

15. Which sentence best describes the narrator in this selection?
   - He enjoys science and travel.
   - He likes to be alone.
   - He does not have any friends.
   - He does not take care of his plants.

STOP

Name ______________________________

REVIEW

Main Idea and Supporting Details

Directions: Read the passage. Then read each question about the passage. Choose the best answer to the question. Mark the space for the answer you have chosen.

Plants and Their Food

All plants make their own food. A plant takes in air and water. The plant's green leaves collect energy from the sun. The plant uses this energy to change the water and part of the air into a kind of sugar. The sugar is food for the plant.

Some plants get food from other places too. People might give plant food to the plants in their garden. Some plants catch and eat small bugs. But all plants can make their own food. That's what makes a plant a plant.

1. This passage tells about—
- ⬭ why plants need water.
- ⬭ plants and their food.
- ⬭ plants that catch animals.
- ⬭ feeding your plants.

2. Plants get the energy to make food from—
- ⬭ dirt
- ⬭ plant food
- ⬭ sunlight
- ⬭ water

3. Which of the following is **not** a source of food for plants?
- ⬭ green leaves
- ⬭ plant food
- ⬭ small bugs
- ⬭ a special sugar that plants make

4. Which of the following is **not** a supporting detail in the passage?
- ⬭ People give plants plant food.
- ⬭ Plants take in air and water.
- ⬭ Some plants eat small bugs.
- ⬭ Some people like to garden.

5. What is something that is true about all plants?
- ⬭ They all make their own food.
- ⬭ They all eat small bugs.
- ⬭ They all grow in gardens.
- ⬭ They all eat plant food.

Notes for Home: Your child answered questions about the main idea and supporting details of a passage. ***Home Activity:*** Read a story or nonfiction article with your child. Have your child summarize its main idea. Then ask your child to name details that support or explain it.

Name ______________________________

Word Study: Compound Words

Directions: Write the two words that make up each compound word on the lines.

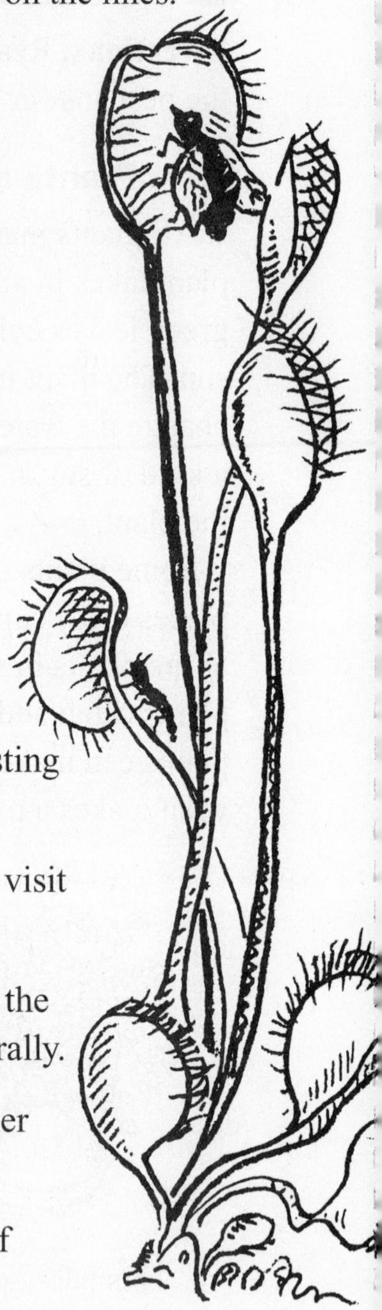

1. __________ + __________ = rainwater
2. __________ + __________ = dewdrop
3. __________ + __________ = sunshine
4. __________ + __________ = milkweed
5. __________ + __________ = sunflower
6. __________ + __________ = treehouse
7. __________ + __________ = outside
8. __________ + __________ = flowerpot

Directions: Choose the compound word to complete each sentence. Write the word on the line.

______________ **9.** The Venus (plant/flytrap) is an interesting meat-eating plant.

______________ **10.** I see these plants (where/whenever) I visit my cousin in Florida.

______________ **11.** In the (northern/southeastern) part of the United States, these plants grow naturally.

______________ **12.** My cousin even has one growing in her (backyard/garden).

______________ **13.** In fact, I wouldn't mind having one of these plants (at home/myself).

______________ **14.** You can leave them on a (windowsill/patio) to catch bugs.

______________ **15.** The plant shop near me keeps some in their (window/greenhouse).

Notes for Home: Your child reviewed compound words—words formed by joining two shorter words—such as *flytrap*. ***Home Activity:*** With your child, read advertisements to find compound words. Have your child identify the two words that make up the compound word.

Name ______________________________

Phonics: Long *i* Spelled *igh, y*; Long *u* Spelled *u-e, u*

REVIEW

Directions: Read each sentence. Say the underlined word in each sentence. Choose the word that has the same vowel sound as the underlined word. Mark the space for the answer you have chosen.

1. The flytrap is an interesting plant.
- windowsill
- high
- into
- may

2. Flytraps grow in the United States.
- sunny
- funnel
- just
- rule

3. I like my meat-eating plants.
- city
- picnic
- light
- hurry

4. It is a hobby I can do by myself.
- tighter
- crayon
- lucky
- body

5. Flytraps use their leaves like traps.
- study
- uncle
- touch
- cute

6. A fly or wasp will often get caught.
- anyone
- myself
- jelly
- journey

7. The leaves close tight around it.
- himself
- cousin
- try
- circle

8. The flytrap is not as huge as a pitcher plant.
- put
- truck
- usual
- uncle

9. The cobra lily has a long tube.
- pull
- music
- muffin
- busy

10. The sundew leaves are like glue.
- under
- lucky
- hurry
- useful

Notes for Home: Your child chose words with long *i* and long *u* vowel sounds. ***Home Activity:*** Read a favorite book with your child and look for words with the same vowel sounds. Ask your child to list the words and study their spellings.

Name ______________________________________

Study Strategies

K-W-L stands for **What I <u>K</u>now, What I <u>W</u>ant to Know,** and **What I <u>L</u>earned.** Before reading, think about questions you have about what you will read. As you read, look for the answers to these questions. You may not be able to answer all of your questions.

Directions: Preview the article below and fill in the first two columns of the table. Then read the article and fill in the third column.

Venus Flytrap

The Venus Flytrap is a plant that grows in a small region in North and South Carolina. It grows in damp, mossy areas. The plant grows to be about 8–12 inches tall and has a cluster of small white flowers at the top. The plant catches small insects in its leaves and digests them. It takes about ten days for the plant to digest an insect. The plant dies after it has digested three or four insects.

Topic ______________________________________

K What I Know	W What I Want to Know	L What I Learned
1.	**3.**	**5.**
2.	**4.**	

Notes for Home: Your child used a K-W-L table to organize information about a topic. ***Home Activity:*** Ask your child to pick a topic of interest. Have him or her use a K-W-L table. Help your child find and read an article about the topic and fill in the table.

Name ______________________________

Realism and Fantasy

- A **realistic story** tells about something that could happen in real life.
- A **fantasy** has some things that could happen and some things that could not happen.

Directions: Reread "Under the Umbrella" and "The Naughty Umbrella." Then complete the tables. Write **Yes** in the second column if the story event could really happen. Write **No** if it could not happen. Then, tell how you know.

"Under the Umbrella"	Yes or No?	How Do You Know?
Ashley sees Rebecca coming down the street.	Yes	**1.**
Rebecca is holding a yellow umbrella.	**2.**	A person can hold a yellow umbrella in real life.
Ashley squeezes close to Rebecca under the umbrella.	Yes	**3.**
The sidewalk is shiny like a gray satin sash.	Yes	**4.**

"The Naughty Umbrella"	Yes or No?	How Do You Know?
The umbrella would pop open and hop around the room.	**5.**	**6.**
The umbrella would try to escape out the window.	**7.**	An umbrella can't move by itself.
Roger would stuff the umbrella into his closet.	Yes	**8.**
The umbrella would thump and flap for hours.	**9.**	**10.**

Notes for Home: Your child identified whether parts of a story could happen in real life. ***Home Activity:*** Help your child understand the meanings of *realism* and *fantasy* by working together to identify events in favorite books as possible or impossible.

Name ________________________________

Vocabulary

Directions: Choose the word from the box that best replaces the underlined word or words. Write the word on the line.

Check the Words You Know

__ breathe
__ dream
__ planet
__ scary
__ space
__ spaceship

_____________ **1.** Have you ever imagined taking a trip into the unlimited area that goes in all directions beyond Earth?

_____________ **2.** Would it be great to travel beyond Earth in a vehicle made for flight into space?

_____________ **3.** You could visit another large body that moves around the Sun!

_____________ **4.** You would need an oxygen tank in order to take air into the lungs and let it out.

_____________ **5.** It might be frightening to be out there in darkness way above Earth.

_____________ **6.** Perhaps it would be better to stay at home and just wish or imagine you flew above Earth.

Directions: Choose the word from the box that best completes each sentence. Write the word on the line to the left.

_____________ **7.** I had a _____ last night while I was sleeping.

_____________ **8.** I imagined I used a _____ to travel to another world.

_____________ **9.** All the people living on the _____ had two heads!

_____________ **10.** At first, I thought they were _____, but they were very friendly. They sure could talk a lot!

Write a Letter

On a separate sheet of paper, write a letter to a friend. Tell your friend about a trip you took into space. Use as many vocabulary words as you can.

Notes for Home: Your child identified and used vocabulary words from *Guys from Space*. ***Home Activity:*** Plan an imaginary space trip with your child. Discuss what it would feel like to travel among the stars. Use vocabulary words in your discussion.

Name ______________________________

Realism and Fantasy

- A **realistic story** tells about something that could happen in real life.
- A **fantasy** has some things that could happen and some things that could not happen.

Directions: Reread what happens in *Guys from Space* when the guys from space land. Then answer the questions below.

When the thing from space had landed, a little door opened.

Guys from space came out.

They were no bigger than me.

"Is this Chicago?" they asked me.

"This is my yard," I said.

The guys from space talked to each other.

"Kid, would you like to come for a ride?"

"No!" I said.

"You don't want to come?"

"No."

"It will be fun," the space guys said. "We will bring you back."

"Nothing doing," I said.

"You will be the first Earth person to ride in our spaceship," they said.

1. Is this sentence a realistic part of the story? Explain.
Guys from space came out.

____

2. Is Chicago a realistic part of the story? Explain. ______________________________

____

3. Could a realistic story have a spaceship? Explain. ______________________________

____

____

4. Rewrite this sentence to make it something that could really happen.
The guys from space talked to each other.

____

5. Is *Guys from Space* a realistic story or a fantasy? Write your answer on a separate sheet of paper. Give examples to support your answer.

Notes for Home: Your child read a story and determined whether the story is realistic or a fantasy. ***Home Activity:*** Watch a television show with your child. Ask your child to identify whether the story is realistic or a fantasy.

Test-Taking Tips

1. Write your name on the test.
2. Read the directions carefully. Make sure you know exactly what you are supposed to do.
3. Read the question twice. Make sure you understand what the question is asking.
4. Read the answer choices for the question. Eliminate choices that do not make sense.
5. Mark your answer carefully.
6. Check your answer. Make sure that it makes the most sense out of all the answer choices.
7. If you have difficulty answering a question, you may want to go on to the next question. You can come back to difficult questions later.
8. If you finish the test early, go back and check all your answers.

Selection Test

Directions: Choose the best answer to each item. Mark the space for the answer you have chosen.

Part 1: Vocabulary

Find the answer choice that means about the same as the underlined word in each sentence.

1. Seth could not <u>breathe</u>.
- take in and let out air
- leave home
- see clearly
- swim in the water

2. We watched a <u>scary</u> movie.
- causing laughter
- boring
- causing fright
- long

3. There are no people on that <u>planet</u>.
- land surrounded by water
- large round body in the sky
- underwater ship
- bridge across a river

4. Have you ever seen a <u>spaceship</u>?
- a vehicle for flight in outer space
- a large boat that crosses the ocean
- a train that runs on a single rail
- a ride in an amusement park

5. It seemed like a <u>dream</u>.
- large airplane
- something from outer space
- good choice
- something seen during sleep

6. The moon moves through <u>space</u>.
- deep water
- large circles of light
- a long road
- the place all around Earth

Part 2: Comprehension

Use what you know about the story to answer each item.

7. Where is the boy at the beginning of the story?
- on a spaceship
- in Chicago
- in his house
- in his backyard

8. What did the boy see in the sky?
- a spaceship
- an airplane
- a bird
- a balloon

GO ON

9. Why didn't the boy's mother go out to see the space guys?
- ⬭ She was making supper.
- ⬭ She did not believe there were any space guys.
- ⬭ She was afraid of them.
- ⬭ She didn't want to scare them away.

10. To ride in the space guys' spaceship, everyone must—
- ⬭ own a dog.
- ⬭ buy a ticket.
- ⬭ wear a helmet.
- ⬭ be at least 12 years old.

11. Why didn't the boy enjoy the ride to another planet?
- ⬭ The spaceship was going too fast.
- ⬭ His helmet was not comfortable.
- ⬭ He was worried he'd get home late.
- ⬭ He didn't trust the space guys.

12. What can you tell about the space guys from this story?
- ⬭ They have lots of money.
- ⬭ They are curious and friendly.
- ⬭ They need to eat and drink often.
- ⬭ They are big and ugly.

13. What part of this story could happen in real life?
- ⬭ A space thing sells root beer.
- ⬭ A spaceship goes to a planet and back in a day.
- ⬭ Space guys eat ice cream.
- ⬭ A boy puts a dog's water bowl on his head.

14. The space guys wanted to hurry back to their own planet to—
- ⬭ keep the ice cream from melting.
- ⬭ be on time for supper.
- ⬭ show the boy where they live.
- ⬭ tell their people about a new treat.

15. What part of this story could **not** really happen?
- ⬭ A boy drinks root beer.
- ⬭ A boy eats ice cream with a spoon.
- ⬭ A rock speaks to a boy.
- ⬭ A boy's mother tells him to wash his hands.

STOP

REVIEW

Sequence

Directions: Read the story. Then read each question about the story. Choose the best answer to the question. Mark the space for the answer you have chosen.

Galaxy One Takes Off

Cody and Nathan wanted to build a spaceship, so they read about what spaceships look like.

First, they gathered cardboard boxes. Then they got tape, scissors, and string. They tied the boxes together with string. They cut holes for windows. Cody's dad gave them wires and switches to make the engine. They decided to name their spaceship the *Galaxy One*.

Soon it was time to try out the spaceship. Suddenly, Cody's dad heard an engine roar and smelled some smoke. All he saw was a hole in the ground. He looked up to the sky. *Galaxy One* was rising high above the treetops! He thought he was dreaming.

1. Before they made the spaceship, Cody and Nathan—
- ⬭ cut holes in the boxes.
- ⬭ named the spaceship.
- ⬭ found an engine for the spaceship.
- ⬭ read about spaceships.

2. The first thing the boys did when they built the spaceship was to—
- ⬭ paint a name on the spaceship.
- ⬭ find cardboard boxes.
- ⬭ decide on a name for the spaceship.
- ⬭ cut holes for the windows.

3. The boys used the scissors to—
- ⬭ make the engine.
- ⬭ paint the name on the spaceship.
- ⬭ tie the boxes together.
- ⬭ cut holes for the windows.

4. After Cody's dad saw a hole in the ground, he—
- ⬭ looked up to the sky.
- ⬭ gave the boys some wires and switches.
- ⬭ heard the engine roar.
- ⬭ smelled some smoke.

5. Which two clue words in the second paragraph help show the sequence of events?
- ⬭ got, cut
- ⬭ first, decided
- ⬭ then, cut
- ⬭ first, then

Notes for Home: Your child read a story and answered questions about the order in which things happened. ***Home Activity:*** Help your child write the order of steps taken to make a favorite sandwich or snack. Then talk about why doing each step in order is important.

Name ________________________________

Phonics: Vowel Digraph oo

Directions: Circle each word with **oo** that has the vowel sound in **book** or the vowel sound in **pool.** Then write each word in the correct column.

1. Our whole class took a field trip to the science museum.
2. The trip was good, and we got out of school at noon.
3. I looked at pictures of the first man to set foot on the moon.
4. Then I stood in line to see the Mars exhibit.
5. Pretty soon, we might send an astronaut to Mars, which will be really cool.

oo as in book	oo as in pool
6. ____________	11. ____________
7. ____________	12. ____________
8. ____________	13. ____________
9. ____________	14. ____________
10. ____________	15. ____________

Directions: Unscramble the letters to form words with a **oo.** Then choose the word that best matches each clue. Write the word on the line.

rombo	sobot	dofo	noso	ozo

____________ **16.** a pair of something you wear on your feet

____________ **17.** a place to visit and see different animals

____________ **18.** what you eat to live and grow

____________ **19.** a short time from now

____________ **20.** something to sweep the floor

Notes for Home: Your child read and wrote words with *oo*. ***Home Activity:*** Look on food packages and other products to find words with *oo.* Ask your child to tell whether the *oo* is pronounced like the vowel sound in *book* or the vowel sound in *pool*.

Name ______________________________

Word Study: Compound Words

REVIEW

Directions: Read each section. Choose the compound word that best completes each sentence. Mark the space for your answer.

1. Today a _____ landed in our yard.
- ⬭ anything
- ⬭ good-bye
- ⬭ spaceship
- ⬭ underground

2. Mom saw _____ and called me.
- ⬭ something
- ⬭ into
- ⬭ leftover
- ⬭ windowsill

3. I ran into the _____.
- ⬭ nothing
- ⬭ whenever
- ⬭ sundew
- ⬭ backyard

4. I didn't see _____ at first.
- ⬭ rainwater
- ⬭ leftover
- ⬭ anything
- ⬭ inside

5. There was _____ around the bushes.
- ⬭ myself
- ⬭ whenever
- ⬭ nothing
- ⬭ outside

6. I asked, "Is _____ there?"
- ⬭ airplane
- ⬭ dewdrops
- ⬭ southeastern
- ⬭ anybody

7. Suddenly, _____ answered me.
- ⬭ afternoon
- ⬭ butterfly
- ⬭ barefoot
- ⬭ someone

8. I looked _____ a bush.
- ⬭ leftover
- ⬭ everything
- ⬭ into
- ⬭ myself

9. There was a small model _____ with a tiny radio inside it.
- ⬭ rainwater
- ⬭ airplane
- ⬭ popcorn
- ⬭ homework

10. _____ laughed when we discovered we had been fooled!
- ⬭ Everyone
- ⬭ Outside
- ⬭ Maybe
- ⬭ Cannot

Notes for Home: Your child chose compound words to complete sentences. ***Home Activity:*** Have your child write the two words in each compound word on index cards. Show one card and ask your child to find the matching card to form a compound word.

Name ______________________________

Alphabetical Order

Entries or subjects in encyclopedias, dictionaries, and indexes are listed in **alphabetical order** so you can find information quickly and easily. When two entries or subjects have the same first letter, alphabetize by the second letter. If the second letters are also the same, alphabetize by the third letter, and so on. See how the entries related to space have been alphabetized in a dictionary.

space age, the current period in history, as marked by the advances made in the exploration of outer space.

space•craft (spās'kraft'), a vehicle or vehicles used for flight in outer space. *noun, plural* **space•craft.**

space•ship (spās'ship'), spacecraft. *noun.*

space shuttle, a spacecraft with wings, which can orbit the earth, land like an airplane, and be used again. A space shuttle has two rockets and a large fuel tank which drop off after use in launching the spacecraft.

space•suit (spās'süt'), an airtight suit that protects travelers in outer space from radiation, heat, and lack of oxygen. *noun.*

space•walk (spās'wȯk'), the act of moving or floating in space while outside a spacecraft. *noun.*

Directions: Put these space-related words in alphabetical order. Use the dictionary example above to help you.

planets	airtight	stars
spacecraft	craters	crust
exploration	air pressure	space

1. ____________ **4.** ____________ **7.** ____________

2. ____________ **5.** ____________ **8.** ____________

3. ____________ **6.** ____________ **9.** ____________

10. If you were looking up the meaning of *special* in a dictionary, would the entry come before or after *spacewalk?* Explain.

____

____

Notes for Home: Your child put words in alphabetical order. ***Home Activity:*** Give your child a list of 10–12 words. Challenge him or her to put them in alphabetical order, or give him or her a stack of books to put on a shelf in alphabetical order.

Name ______________________________

Context Clues

- To figure out the meaning of a word, use **context clues.**
- Often a context clue defines or explains the word. Look in the sentences or the paragraph around the word.
- You may need to use a dictionary or glossary to check the meaning of the word.

Directions: Reread "Stormy Weather." Use context clues from the selection to define each word below.

Word	Meaning
hurricanes	**1.**
eye	**2.**
typhoons	**3.**
tornadoes	**4.**
column	**5.**

Notes for Home: Your child used context clues to help define words. ***Home Activity:*** Encourage your child to keep a list of unfamiliar words he or she finds while reading. Discuss how context clues can be used to help figure out the meaning of each word.

Name ____________________________________

Vocabulary

Directions: Choose the word from the box that best completes each sentence. Write the word on the line to the left.

Check the Words You Know

__ destroy
__ noise
__ powerful
__ storms
__ warnings
__ wrecked

________________ **1.** _____ can bring rain, hail, and high winds.

________________ **2.** They can tear apart and _____ cars, homes, and even large buildings.

________________ **3.** They can be so strong and _____ that entire towns are damaged.

________________ **4.** Weather forecasters give _____ so people can take shelter and protect homes.

Directions: Choose the word from the box that best matches each clue. Write the word in the puzzle.

Across

5. strong; forceful

7. smashed; torn down

9. unpleasant sound

10. strong winds and rains

Down

6. things that tell about danger

8. ruin

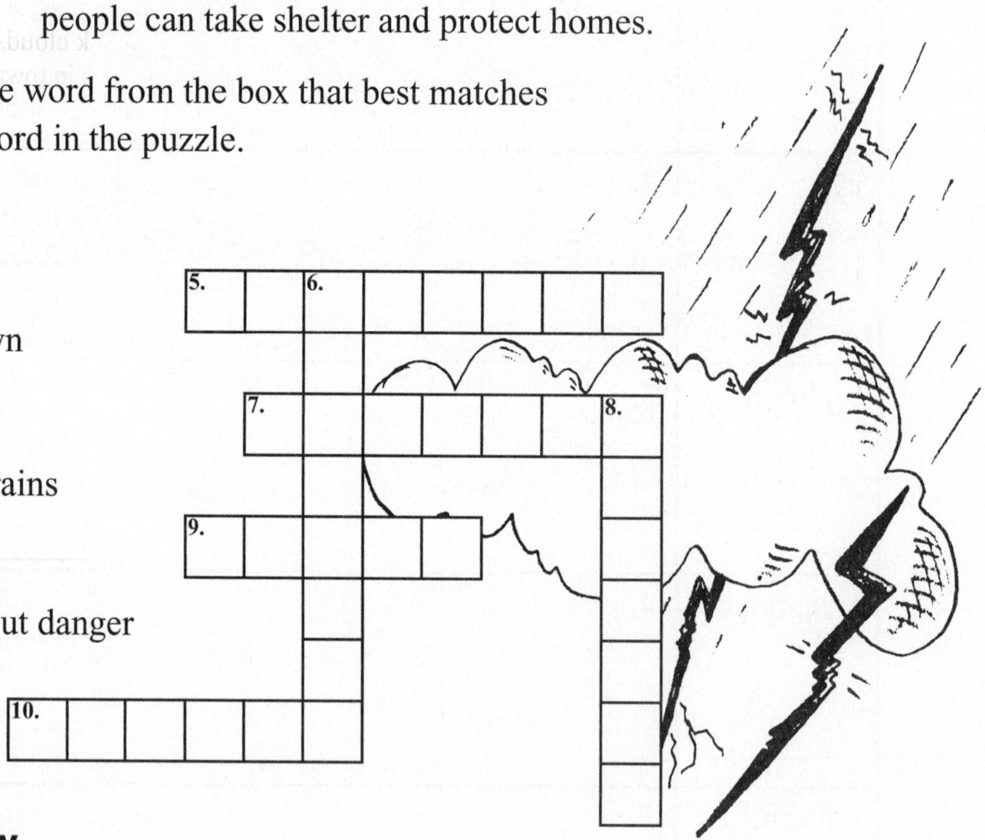

Write a News Story

Imagine you are a writer for the local TV news. On a separate sheet of paper, write a story about a storm in your city or town. Use as many of the vocabulary words as possible.

Notes for Home: Your child identified and used vocabulary words from *Tornado Alert*. ***Home Activity:*** Ask your child to tell you about a storm he or she has experienced. Encourage your child to use as many vocabulary words as possible.

Name ______________________________

Context Clues

- To figure out the meaning of a word, use **context clues.**
- Often a context clue defines or explains the word. Look in the sentences or the paragraph around the word.
- You may need to use a dictionary or glossary to check the meaning of the word.

Directions: Reread this part of *Tornado Alert* that describes a tornado forming. Then answer the questions below.

The cold air pushes under the warm air. The warm air is lighter than the cold air and rises rapidly.

As the warm air moves upward, it spins around, or twists. That's why tornadoes are sometimes called twisters. Some people call them cyclones. The wind speed around the funnel of the tornado may reach 300 miles an hour. No other wind on Earth blows that fast.

As the hot air rises, it also spreads out. It makes a funnel of air, with the small part of the funnel touching the ground and the large part in the dark clouds. Air all around the tornado moves in toward the funnel. At the same time, storm winds push the twisting funnel, moving it along the Earth.

1. What is a twister? ______________________________

____

2. What is a cyclone? ______________________________

____

3. What is a funnel? ______________________________

____

4. What clues help you picture what a funnel is? ______________________________

____

5. Use the context clues in *Tornado Alert* to write a definition of the word *tornado*. Write your definition on a separate sheet of paper.

Notes for Home: Your child read a nonfiction selection and used context clues to define words. ***Home Activity:*** Read a newspaper article with your child. Help him or her use context clues to figure out the meaning of any unfamiliar words.

Test-Taking Tips

1. Write your name on the test.
2. Read the directions carefully. Make sure you know exactly what you are supposed to do.
3. Read the question twice. Make sure you understand what the question is asking.
4. Read the answer choices for the question. Eliminate choices that do not make sense.
5. Mark your answer carefully.
6. Check your answer. Make sure that it makes the most sense out of all the answer choices.
7. If you have difficulty answering a question, you may want to go on to the next question. You can come back to difficult questions later.
8. If you finish the test early, go back and check all your answers.

Name ______________________________

Selection Test

Directions: Choose the best answer to each item. Mark the space for the answer you have chosen.

Part 1: Vocabulary

Find the answer choice that means about the same as the underlined word in each sentence.

1. A powerful wind blew across the plain.
   - hot and dry
   - gentle
   - warm and pleasant
   - strong

2. You make a lot of noise.
   - anything that can be seen
   - musical notes
   - loud, unpleasant sound
   - something that makes people laugh

3. This rain will destroy our crops.
   - ruin
   - soak
   - improve
   - feed

4. Lyn drove through the storms.
   - flat lands covered with grass
   - ditches beside a road
   - strong winds and rain
   - bright lights

5. There were three warnings today.
   - gifts given to someone
   - notices given in advance
   - events that cause damage
   - rules to be followed

6. The wind wrecked our house.
   - moved from side to side
   - made more beautiful
   - came near
   - tore apart

Part 2: Comprehension

Use what you know about the selection to answer each item.

7. Tornadoes most often occur over—
   - mountains.
   - flat land.
   - bodies of water.
   - cities and towns.

8. Which is the best safety rule to follow during a tornado?
   - Always wear a seat belt.
   - Hold on to something, such as a telephone pole.
   - Stay low and away from windows.
   - Stand in a flat, open place.

GO ON

9. During a tornado, what causes most of the noise?
- freight trains
- jet engines
- thunder
- wind

10. What can you tell about tornadoes from this selection?
- They can be very dangerous.
- They are mostly all the same.
- They will not hurt you.
- They are not as strong as people think.

11. You can tell from the clues in this selection that a waterspout is a kind of—
- thunderstorm.
- tornado.
- lake.
- cloud.

12. Why does the author tell you to listen to a battery radio?
- Batteries do not get wet.
- The electricity might go off.
- Battery radios get more stations.
- Batteries are stronger than electricity.

13. Why isn't it safe to talk on the telephone during a tornado?
- A telephone pole might fall on you.
- Someone might need to call you.
- Lightning can hit the telephone wires.
- Thunder can hurt your ears.

14. The author's purpose in this selection is to—
- tell an entertaining story.
- give information about tornadoes.
- explain how lightning works.
- describe the weather in Texas.

15. Where is the safest place to be during a tornado?
- in a tent
- in an airplane
- in a mobile home
- in a basement

STOP

Name ______________________________

Graphic Sources

REVIEW

Directions: Read the passage and the table. Then read each question about the passage and the table. Choose the best answer to the question. Mark the space for the answer you have chosen.

Safe in a Tornado

Since a tornado can happen almost anywhere, it is a good idea to know how to be safe if a tornado strikes. The table gives some safety tips.

In School
Follow teacher's instructions. Go to a safe place without many windows. Cover your head with your hands.
At Home
Go to the basement, into a closet, under stairs, or under large furniture. Have a flashlight, battery radio, candles, matches, and water handy. Wait until the storm has passed before leaving your safe place.
Outside
Find shelter. Lie down in a ditch or enclosed area. Cover your head with your hands. Stay away from trees and water. Do not stay in a car.

1. This table is about safety in—
- ⊂⊃ school, at home, and outside.
- ⊂⊃ a shelter, a closet, and a car.
- ⊂⊃ a basement, a car, and a ditch.
- ⊂⊃ your school and home.

2. At home, it is important to—
- ⊂⊃ lie down in a ditch.
- ⊂⊃ have a flashlight and batteries.
- ⊂⊃ stay away from trees.
- ⊂⊃ follow your teacher's instructions.

3. If you are outside when a tornado strikes, you must never—
- ⊂⊃ get away from trees.
- ⊂⊃ cover your head.
- ⊂⊃ stay in a car.
- ⊂⊃ go into a ditch.

4. In school, you may have to—
- ⊂⊃ have a flashlight.
- ⊂⊃ cover your head.
- ⊂⊃ lie down in a ditch.
- ⊂⊃ get away from water.

5. What is a good title for this table?
- ⊂⊃ School and Home Safety
- ⊂⊃ Tornado Safety in School
- ⊂⊃ Tornado Safety
- ⊂⊃ Tornadoes

Notes for Home: Your child answered questions about a table. ***Home Activity:*** Help your child make a table or diagram of fire safety plans for your home. List or show the locations of exit doors, stairways, a fire extinguisher, and other fire safety devices.

Name ___________________________________

Phonics: Vowel Digraph *ou*; Diphthong *ou*

Directions: Circle all the words with the same vowel sound as the first word.

1. house	hour	ground	though	mouse
2. should	soup	touch	could	would
3. you	about	soup	through	ounce
4. loud	shout	could	mouth	round
5. about	scout	would	tough	sound

Directions: Choose the word from the box that best completes each sentence. Hint: It has the same vowel sound as the underlined word. Write the word on the line to the left.

cloud	could	out	through	underground

_______________ **6.** When we heard the sound of the tornado, we got ready to go to our _____ shelter.

_______________ **7.** The noise started getting loud. Then we saw the funnel _____.

_______________ **8.** I heard my dad shout for all of us to get _____ of the house.

_______________ **9.** We all knew that we should move as fast as we _____.

_______________ **10.** Tornadoes can be scary, but you can get _____ them okay if you go to a safe place.

Notes for Home: Your child reviewed words with *ou* and the different vowel sounds *ou* represents. ***Home Activity:*** Look through a newspaper with your child for words with *ou*. Ask your child to tell you whether the *ou* is pronounced like *shout, should, you,* or *touch*.

Name ______________________________

Phonics: Vowel Digraph *oo*

REVIEW

Directions: Read each sentence. Say the underlined word in each sentence. Choose the word that has the same vowel sound as the underlined word. Mark the space for your answer.

1. Dad said goodbye and got on the train.
- ⬭ soon
- ⬭ moon
- ⬭ looked
- ⬭ balloon

2. Mom took the car to work.
- ⬭ good
- ⬭ dog
- ⬭ too
- ⬭ pool

3. Grandma came to my bedroom.
- ⬭ flood
- ⬭ pole
- ⬭ shook
- ⬭ rule

4. I was too late for the bus.
- ⬭ book
- ⬭ boot
- ⬭ good
- ⬭ shook

5. My school is not far from home.
- ⬭ cookie
- ⬭ stool
- ⬭ stood
- ⬭ foot

6. I ran into the classroom.
- ⬭ balloon
- ⬭ blood
- ⬭ took
- ⬭ wood

7. Suddenly rain came through the roof.
- ⬭ sport
- ⬭ spot
- ⬭ spoon
- ⬭ out

8. We looked for a leak.
- ⬭ fool
- ⬭ gloomy
- ⬭ soup
- ⬭ shook

9. We worried the room might flood.
- ⬭ fool
- ⬭ blood
- ⬭ roof
- ⬭ room

10. We stood in the hall while the leak was fixed.
- ⬭ stone
- ⬭ balloon
- ⬭ foot
- ⬭ popcorn

Notes for Home: Your child reviewed words with *oo* that represent the vowel sounds heard in *took, soon,* and *flood*. ***Home Activity:*** Write the words with *oo* shown above on slips of paper. Take turns picking a word and saying a word that rhymes.

Name ______________________________

Almanac

An **almanac** is a yearly book that contains calendars, weather information, dates of holidays, and charts and tables of current information on many subjects.

Directions: Study these tables from an almanac below. Then answer the questions.

Average Temperatures High/Low (January)		
State	**City**	**Hi/Lo**
Alabama	Mobile	60/40
California	San Diego	66/49
Florida	Miami	75/59
Texas	Houston	61/40
Wisconsin	Milwaukee	26/12

Wind Speed (mi/hr) 1995	
City, State	**Average/High**
Anchorage, AK	7.1/75
Buffalo, NY	11.9/91
Chicago, IL	10.4/58
Denver, CO	8.6/46
Mt. Washington, NH	35.3/231

1. Which city had the lowest average temperature for January? ______________

2. In which city would you expect to find snow in January? Explain.

____

____

3. Which city had the highest wind speeds in 1995? ______________

4. Chicago had a high wind speed of 58 mi/hr. Do you think it is that windy in Chicago every day? Explain.

____

____

5. Suppose you were writing a report on the weather in your state. How might you use weather data found in an almanac in your report?

____

____

Notes for Home: Your child read weather data and answered questions about it. ***Home Activity:*** Help your child read an almanac that gives information about where you live. Discuss how the information found in almanacs can be used to describe your area.

Name ______________________________

Fact and Opinion

- A **statement of fact** can be proved true or false.
- A **statement of opinion** is what someone believes or thinks. There may or may not be a good reason to think this way.
- Words that express what someone feels or thinks, such as *believe, like,* and *should,* are clues that a statement is an opinion.

Directions: Reread "About Sharks." Then read each statement and decide if it is fact or opinion. Write an **X** in the correct column.

Statement	Fact	Opinion
1. Sharks live in every neighborhood of the ocean, from warm tropic waters to the chilly depths.		
2. The Greenland sharks live among and beneath the Arctic Ice.		
3. I spent 11,000 hours underwater.		
4. I like sharks.		
5. I believe sharks are worth saving.		
6. Sharks eat weak and sick fish.		
7. Fish are a source of food for humans and livestock.		
8. Fish meal is used to make cattle and chicken feed.		
9. Sharks are good to eat.		
10. Shark skeletons are made of cartilage.		

Notes for Home: Your child identified information as either statements of fact or opinion. ***Home Activity:*** Make up a sentence or read one from a book. Ask your child to tell you whether it is a statement of fact or opinion, and why.

Vocabulary

Directions: Choose the word from the box that best completes each sentence. Write the word on the line to the left.

Check the Words You Know

__ alert
__ breaks
__ melt
__ ocean
__ thousands

_______________ **1.** We are sailing across the _____.

_______________ **2.** The ship is so big, it holds _____ of people.

_______________ **3.** A huge wave _____ when it hits the bow of the ship.

_______________ **4.** It is so cold where we are that snow and ice do not _____.

_______________ **5.** The crew must always stay _____ and watch out for icebergs.

Directions: The first sentence of each pair is a clue. Choose the word from the box that best completes the second sentence. Write the word on the line to the left.

_______________ **6.** When water gets cold, it will freeze. When ice gets hot, it will _____.

_______________ **7.** Many tens make hundreds. Many hundreds make _____.

_______________ **8.** Fresh water is found in most lakes. Salt water is found in the _____.

_______________ **9.** You sew something when it rips. You fix something when it _____.

_______________ **10.** When you are tired, you are drowsy. When you are awake, you are _____.

Write a Riddle

On a separate sheet of paper, write a riddle for each vocabulary word. Such as: (I'm loud and I'll make you cover your ears. What am I? Noise!)

Notes for Home: Your child identified and used vocabulary words from *Danger—Icebergs!* ***Home Activity:*** Pretend that you are the captain of a ship, and your child is a crew member. Discuss what course the ship should take, using vocabulary words.

Name ______________________________

Fact and Opinion

- A **statement of fact** can be proved true or false.
- A **statement of opinion** is what someone believes or thinks. There may or may not be a good reason to think this way.
- Words that express what someone feels or thinks, such as *believe, like,* and *should,* are clues that a statement is an opinion.

Directions: Reread this description of the *Titanic* from *Danger—Icebergs!* Then answer the questions below.

> Even strong modern ships have struck bergs. One such crash happened in April 1912. A ship called the *Titanic* sailed from England on its first voyage. "Titanic" means large. The ship was the biggest and most beautiful ship ever built. No storms or icebergs could sink it—or so people said.
>
>

1. Is the following sentence a fact or an opinion? Explain.
Even strong modern ships have struck bergs.

____

2. Is the following sentence a fact or an opinion? Explain.
A ship called the Titanic *sailed from England on its first voyage.*

____

3. The following sentence contains a statement of fact. What is it?
The ship was the biggest and most beautiful ship ever built.

____

4. The sentence also contains a statement of opinion. What is it?
The ship was the biggest and most beautiful ship ever built.

____

5. Does *Danger—Icebergs!* present mostly facts or mostly opinions? Explain your answer on a separate sheet of paper.

Notes for Home: Your child identified statements of fact and opinion. ***Home Activity:*** Work with your child to identify some statements of fact and opinion in a school newsletter or the local newspaper. Look at advertisements or letters to the editor for statements of opinion.

Test-Taking Tips

1. Write your name on the test.
2. Read the directions carefully. Make sure you know exactly what you are supposed to do.
3. Read the question twice. Make sure you understand what the question is asking.
4. Read the answer choices for the question. Eliminate choices that do not make sense.
5. Mark your answer carefully.
6. Check your answer. Make sure that it makes the most sense out of all the answer choices.
7. If you have difficulty answering a question, you may want to go on to the next question. You can come back to difficult questions later.
8. If you finish the test early, go back and check all your answers.

Name ______________________________

Selection Test

Directions: Choose the best answer to each item. Mark the space for the answer you have chosen.

Part 1: Vocabulary

Find the answer choice that means about the same as the underlined word in each sentence.

1. Do you live near the <u>ocean</u>?
- ⬭ a place where airplanes land
- ⬭ land surrounded by water
- ⬭ a large mass of ice
- ⬭ a large body of salt water

2. The baby was very <u>alert</u>.
- ⬭ comfortable
- ⬭ sleepy
- ⬭ watchful
- ⬭ grumpy

3. The ice <u>breaks</u> in the spring.
- ⬭ comes apart
- ⬭ rests on top of water
- ⬭ sticks out
- ⬭ freezes

4. The snow will <u>melt</u> soon.
- ⬭ begin to fall
- ⬭ turn into liquid
- ⬭ become hard
- ⬭ move forward

5. <u>Thousands</u> watched the game.
- ⬭ ten dozens
- ⬭ large families
- ⬭ ten hundreds
- ⬭ groups

Part 2: Comprehension

Use what you know about the selection to answer each item.

6. Deep cracks in a glacier are caused by—
- ⬭ ice packs.
- ⬭ ocean waves.
- ⬭ polar bears.
- ⬭ loud roars.

7. Why do ships stay far away from icebergs?
- ⬭ Icebergs make the water cold.
- ⬭ The sailors don't want to scare the animals living there.
- ⬭ The largest part of an iceberg is hidden below the water.
- ⬭ Icebergs often flip over and cause waves.

8. A loud boom heard near an iceberg would most likely be caused by—
- ⬭ a ship running into an iceberg.
- ⬭ a bubble of air in an iceberg breaking.
- ⬭ a berg scraping land.
- ⬭ a bear or seal yelping.

GO ON

9. Unlike the ships of today, wooden ships that sailed hundreds of years ago did not have—
- ⬭ radar.
- ⬭ watchmen.
- ⬭ sails.
- ⬭ passengers.

10. In April 1912, which event happened first?
- ⬭ The *Titanic* hit an iceberg.
- ⬭ Lifeboats were lowered.
- ⬭ Captain E. J. Smith received warnings about icebergs.
- ⬭ Seams in the ship's hull began to give way.

11. When the *Titanic* hit an iceberg, people were not scared at first because—
- ⬭ Captain Smith told them there was no reason to be scared.
- ⬭ they believed that nothing could sink the *Titanic.*
- ⬭ Captain Smith sent an SOS.
- ⬭ they were close to land.

12. What did you learn about small bergs from reading this selection?
- ⬭ Small bergs are not dangerous.
- ⬭ Most small bergs come from glaciers in Greenland.
- ⬭ They usually travel with many larger bergs.
- ⬭ Even a small berg can sink a large ship.

13. Which sentence states an opinion?
- ⬭ Even strong modern ships have struck bergs.
- ⬭ The *Titanic* was the most beautiful ship ever built.
- ⬭ The *Titanic* sailed from England on its first voyage.
- ⬭ One crash happened in April 1912.

14. Which sentence states a fact?
- ⬭ Icebergs are beautiful.
- ⬭ Thousands of icebergs break off from glaciers each year.
- ⬭ People should learn more about icebergs.
- ⬭ There is too much ice in the ocean.

15. What was the most serious result of the *Titanic* disaster?
- ⬭ People became afraid of icebergs.
- ⬭ Three years of work was wasted.
- ⬭ A huge amount of money was lost.
- ⬭ More than 1,500 people died.

STOP

Author's Purpose

REVIEW

Directions: Read the passage. Then read each question about the passage. Choose the best answer to the question. Mark the space for the answer you have chosen.

The Oceans and the Food We Eat

The Pacific, Atlantic, and Indian Oceans cover about seventy percent of the earth's surface. We need the oceans for many things, but one of the most important is for food. Some of the food that we get from the ocean includes lobster, shrimp, and many kinds of fish. Some people even eat seaweed.

Oceans also help give us food that doesn't come out of the ocean. They help food crops on land grow by helping make rain. Water from the ocean changes into clouds, and winds carry the clouds across land. Clouds give the rain that the earth needs to grow the food that you eat. During your next meal, think about the important role that the huge oceans of the world play in giving us the food we need.

1. Which sentence tells what the passage is all about?
- ⬭ Fish live in the ocean.
- ⬭ Rain comes from clouds.
- ⬭ Oceans are very big.
- ⬭ Oceans give people food in different ways.

2. What did you learn about oceans helping grow food on land?
- ⬭ Oceans help create the rain that crops need to grow.
- ⬭ Oceans provide sunshine to help crops grow.
- ⬭ Fish live in the ocean.
- ⬭ Some people like to eat fish.

3. The author wrote this passage to—
- ⬭ explain how rain helps food to grow.
- ⬭ explain how big the oceans are.
- ⬭ explain how oceans help give us the food we eat.
- ⬭ convince us to eat seafood.

4. The passage is—
- ⬭ funny.
- ⬭ sad.
- ⬭ full of information.
- ⬭ mysterious.

5. Who do you think might have been the author of this story?
- ⬭ a scientist who studies oceans
- ⬭ a poet
- ⬭ an actor
- ⬭ a person who likes fishing

Notes for Home: Your child identified the author's purpose for a passage—the reason or reasons an author has for writing. ***Home Activity:*** Look through a variety of print material with your child. Talk about why someone wrote each kind of text.

Name ____________________________________

Phonics: Consonants *j* and *g* /j/; Consonants *s* and *c* /s/

Directions: Read the paragraph. Circle all the underlined words with the consonants **j** and **g** that have the sound /j/ as in **stranger** and **jar.** Write the words on the lines below.

We're going to read a story today. It tells about things that really happened long ago. It is a tale full of danger and courage. It happened on an old sailing ship. The ship carried gold and jewels, and gems from far-off cities. The sailors had been on a seven year journey. They didn't know their voyage would end in tragedy. We will be reading the original journal written by the captain himself.

1. ________________ **4.** ________________ **7.** ________________

2. ________________ **5.** ________________ **8.** ________________

3. ________________ **6.** ________________ **9.** ________________

Directions: Read the paragraph. Circle all the underlined words with the consonants **s** and **c** that have the sound /s/ as in the words **song** and **city.** Write the words on the lines below.

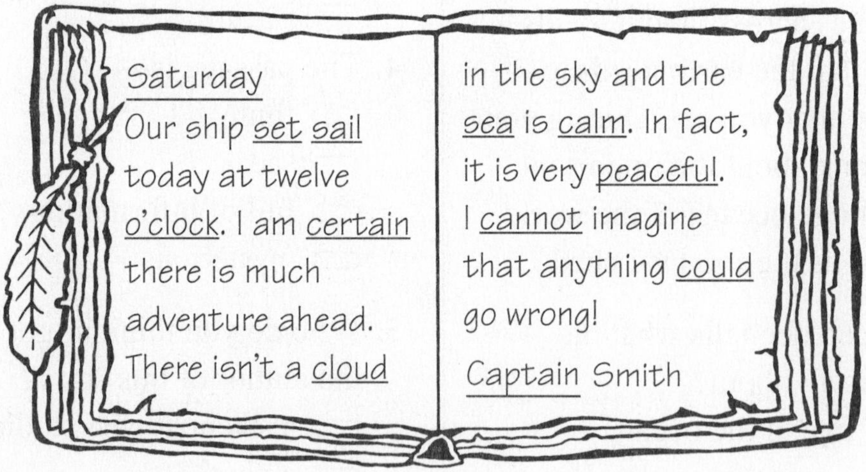

Saturday
Our ship set sail
today at twelve
o'clock. I am certain
there is much
adventure ahead.
There isn't a cloud
in the sky and the
sea is calm. In fact,
it is very peaceful.
I cannot imagine
that anything could
go wrong!
Captain Smith

10. ________________ **13.** ________________

11. ________________ **14.** ________________

12. ________________ **15.** ________________

Notes for Home: Your child reviewed words with the consonants *j* and *g* that have the sound /j/ heard in *stranger* and *jar* and the consonants *s* and *c* that have the sound /s/ heard in *song* and *city*. ***Home Activity:*** Work with your child to list other words that have these consonant sounds.

Name ____

Phonics: Long *a* and *o* Digraphs; Long *o* spelled *o*

REVIEW

Directions: Read each sentence. Choose the word with the long vowel sound that best completes each sentence. Mark the space for your answer.

1. We are going to the shore ____.
- ⬭ soon
- ⬭ now
- ⬭ today
- ⬭ ago

2. I'll take a ____ to the beach.
- ⬭ ball
- ⬭ pail
- ⬭ towel
- ⬭ shovel

3. I like to ____ at the beach.
- ⬭ play
- ⬭ jump
- ⬭ run
- ⬭ go

4. We sail on the ocean in our new ____.
- ⬭ ship
- ⬭ canoe
- ⬭ rainbow
- ⬭ sailboat

5. Last year we ____ our motor boat.
- ⬭ sold
- ⬭ wrecked
- ⬭ lost
- ⬭ mailed

6. Dad and I ____ the new boat.
- ⬭ played
- ⬭ love
- ⬭ painted
- ⬭ also

7. I help Dad ____ the sails.
- ⬭ set
- ⬭ lift
- ⬭ cut
- ⬭ raise

8. We listen to the ____.
- ⬭ wind
- ⬭ radio
- ⬭ gulls
- ⬭ almost

9. We can see the ____ as we sail away.
- ⬭ land
- ⬭ houses
- ⬭ sofas
- ⬭ coast

10. It's ____ if the wind is calm.
- ⬭ best
- ⬭ good
- ⬭ okay
- ⬭ better

Notes for Home: Your child reviewed words with long *a* (*pail, say*) and long *o* (*boat, most*). ***Home Activity:*** Have your child find all the words with long *a* and long *o* sounds on this page. Sort the words by their spellings. Some words may have both vowel sounds.

Name ______________________________

Dictionary

A **dictionary** is a book of words and their meanings. **Guide words** are printed in large, dark type at the top of each dictionary page. They show the first and last words printed on the page.

Directions: Use the dictionary page to answer the questions.

fish/flagpole

fish (fish), **1** one of a group of cold-blooded animals with a long backbone that lives in water and have gills instead of lungs. Fish are usually covered with scales and have fins for swimming. Some kinds of fish lay eggs in the water; others produce living young. **2** the flesh of fish used for food. **3** to catch fish; try to catch fish. **4** to search: *I fished in my pocket for a dime.* **5** to find and pull: *She fished the map from the drawer.* 1, 2 *noun, plural* **fish** or **fish•es;** 3–5 *verb.*

fish•hook (fish′ hu̇k′), a hook used for catching fish. *noun.*

fishy (fish′ē), **1** like a fish in smell, taste, or shape. **2** doubtful; unlikely: *That story sounds fishy; I don't believe it. adjective,* **fish•i•er, fish•i•est.**

1. What are the guide words for this page? ______________________________

2. Find the entry word *fish.* Write the meaning of *fish* as it is used in this sentence: *She fished in her purse to find her car keys.*

____

3. If *fisherman* were an entry word on this page, between which two entry words would it be found?

____

4. Find the second dictionary meaning for the word *fishy.* Use *fishy* in a sentence.

____

____

5. Would you look in a dictionary to find out how to cook fish? Explain.

____

Notes for Home: Your child read entries in a dictionary and used them to answer questions. ***Home Activity:*** Choose two words from a story or magazine that your child doesn't know. Challenge your child to find the words in a dictionary and then use each word correctly in a sentence.

Name ______________________________

Main Idea and Supporting Details

- The **main idea** is the most important idea of a paragraph. A main idea is sometimes stated in the paragraph.
- **Supporting details** are small pieces of information in the paragraph that tell more about the main idea.

Directions: Reread "Shapes and Sizes of Sea Birds." Then complete the table by telling the main idea of a paragraph and some of its supporting details. The first paragraph has been done for you.

Paragraph	Main Idea	Supporting Details
Paragraph 1	Sea birds' bodies have different shapes, but all are streamlined.	Albatrosses, penguins, and pelicans are stout. Terns and petrels are slender.
Paragraph 2	**1.**	The least storm petrel is 13 cm (5 in.) long. The largest albatross has a wing span of more than 360 cm (12 ft.). **2.**
Paragraph 3	**3.**	**4.** **5.**

Notes for Home: Your child identified the main ideas and supporting details in paragraphs of an article. ***Home Activity:*** Help your child write supporting details for a sentence you give as the main idea. For example: *Picnics are fun. (You eat outdoors. You eat good food.)*

Name ______________________________

Vocabulary

Directions: The first sentence of each pair is a clue. Choose the word from the box that best completes the second sentence. Write the word on the line to the left.

Check the Words You Know
__ burrows
__ cardboard
__ cliff
__ hatch
__ island
__ searching
__ underground

______________ **1.** A plane flies overhead. A subway travels _____.

______________ **2.** A dress is made of cloth. A box is made of _____.

______________ **3.** Kittens are born. Ducklings _____.

Directions: Choose the word from the box that best matches each clue. Write the word in the puzzle.

Across

4. come out from an egg

8. beneath the surface of the ground

9. a very steep slope of rock

10. a body of land surrounded by water

Down

5. stiff, light material used to make cartons and boxes

6. holes dug in the ground by an animal for protection or shelter

7. looking carefully for something

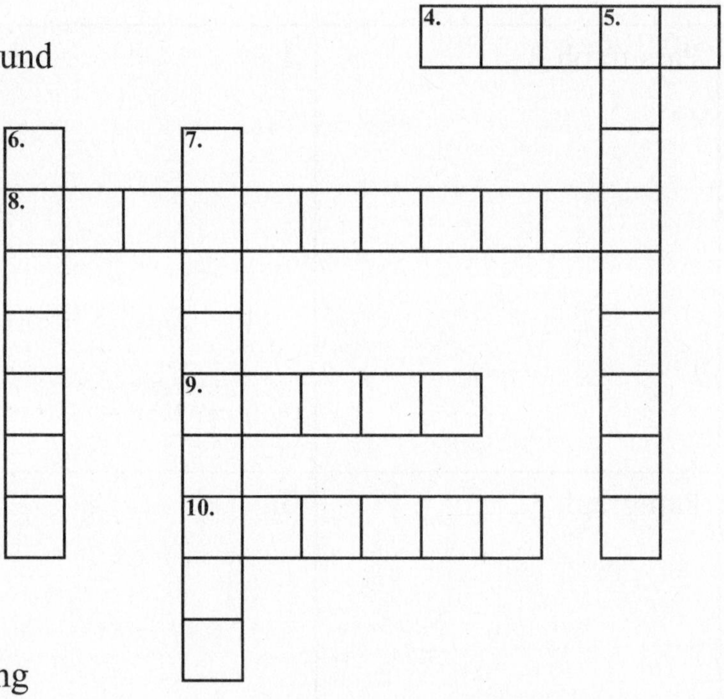

Write a Story

Write a story about rescuing an animal or bird. Use as many vocabulary words as you can.

Notes for Home: Your child identified and used vocabulary words from *Nights of the Pufflings.* ***Home Activity:*** Go for a walk with your child. Look for animals together. Talk about ways to help animals and birds survive. Use as many of the vocabulary words as possible.

Name ______________________________

Main Idea and Supporting Details

- The **main idea** is the most important idea of a paragraph. A main idea is sometimes stated in the paragraph.
- **Supporting details** are small pieces of information in the paragraph that tell more about the main idea.

Directions: Reread this part of *Nights of the Pufflings,* which tells what the children do to rescue pufflings. Then answer the questions below.

Halla and her friends race to the rescue. Armed with their flashlights, they wander through the village. They search dark places. Halla yells out "puffling" in Icelandic. "Lundi pysja!" *(LOON • dah PEESH • yar)* She has spotted one. When the puffling runs down the street, she races after it, grabs it, and nestles it in her arms. Arnar Ingi catches one, too. No sooner are the pufflings safe in the cardboard boxes than more of them land nearby. "Lundi pysja! Lundi pysja!"

1. What is the main idea of this paragraph?

____

____

2. Is the main idea of this paragraph stated in the paragraph? Explain.

____

3.–4. Give two supporting details from the paragraph.

____

____

____

5. What is the main idea of *Nights of the Pufflings?* Write your answer on a separate sheet of paper.

Notes for Home: Your child read and identified the main idea and supporting details of a nonfiction passage and a whole selection. ***Home Activity:*** Pick a paragraph from a story you have read with your child. Ask your child to identify its main idea and some supporting details.

Test-Taking Tips

1. Write your name on the test.
2. Read the directions carefully. Make sure you know exactly what you are supposed to do.
3. Read the question twice. Make sure you understand what the question is asking.
4. Read the answer choices for the question. Eliminate choices that do not make sense.
5. Mark your answer carefully.
6. Check your answer. Make sure that it makes the most sense out of all the answer choices.
7. If you have difficulty answering a question, you may want to go on to the next question. You can come back to difficult questions later.
8. If you finish the test early, go back and check all your answers.

Name ________________________________

Selection Test

Directions: Choose the best answer to each item. Mark the space for the answer you have chosen.

Part 1: Vocabulary

Find the answer choice that means about the same as the underlined word in each sentence.

1. Anna stood on a <u>cliff</u>.
- ⬭ a very steep hill
- ⬭ a large wooden box
- ⬭ a kind of step stool
- ⬭ the top of a lighthouse

2. Hundreds of chicks will <u>hatch</u>.
- ⬭ hunt for food
- ⬭ grow wings
- ⬭ come out of eggs
- ⬭ learn to fly

3. The police are <u>searching</u> for clues.
- ⬭ working hard
- ⬭ looking carefully
- ⬭ flying low
- ⬭ calling loudly

4. Some animals live <u>underground</u>.
- ⬭ in the trees
- ⬭ in the same place
- ⬭ a long time
- ⬭ beneath the earth's surface

5. Many birds live on that <u>island</u>.
- ⬭ small body of land surrounded by water
- ⬭ large nest
- ⬭ small group of trees
- ⬭ bush with red berries

6. These <u>burrows</u> have been here for years.
- ⬭ small carts with wheels
- ⬭ holes in the ground
- ⬭ long-legged birds
- ⬭ large pieces of metal

7. Liam found a <u>cardboard</u> box.
- ⬭ rock formed from mud that has become hard
- ⬭ strong board made of thin layers of wood glued together
- ⬭ a bunch of metal threads twisted together
- ⬭ stiff material made of layers of paper

Part 2: Comprehension

Use what you know about the selection to answer each item.

8. *Lundi* is the Icelandic word for—
- ⬭ clown.
- ⬭ island.
- ⬭ puffin.
- ⬭ chick.

GO ON

9. Who are the "clowns of the sea" mentioned in this selection?
- the puffins
- Halla and her friends
- the children of Heimaey
- seals and otters

10. Pairs of puffins "talk" to each other by—
- flapping their wings.
- taking care of eggs.
- stamping their feet.
- tapping their beaks together.

11. How do Halla and her friends know there are chicks in the burrows?
- They can hear the chicks calling.
- They can see the chicks.
- The chicks come out to swim in the ocean.
- The chicks eat fish that the children put out for them.

12. The children use cardboard boxes to—
- collect puffin eggs.
- catch cats in the village.
- carry pufflings to the beach.
- sit on when they get tired.

13. What can you tell from this selection about the children of Heimaey Island?
- They are cruel to animals.
- They care about nature.
- They are not very good students.
- They like to sleep late.

14. What would be another good title for this selection?
- "Lazy Summer Days on an Island"
- "The Villages of Iceland"
- "Puffling Rescue on Heimaey Island"
- "The Children of Iceland"

15. Which sentence tells what this selection is mostly about?
- Every summer, Icelandic children work hard to help the pufflings survive.
- Dogs and cats pose a great danger to pufflings.
- Puffins make large nests where chicks will be safe all summer.
- Puffins come ashore to have chicks and then fly out to sea.

STOP

Summarizing

REVIEW

Directions: Read the passage. Then read each question about the passage. Choose the best answer to the question. Mark the space for the answer you have chosen.

The Beak of the Puffin

The puffin's beak helps this sea bird in many ways. The beak is like a hook, and it quickly catches and holds fish. A puffin can catch and hold many fish in its beak while it swims underwater.

The puffin's beak also is used as a shovel to dig into the earth and to push and pull rocks.

While the puffin's beak is grayish brown most of the year, it grows a bright cover in the spring. The colors of this cover are bright red, blue, and gold. These colorful beaks help draw the attention of a mate.

1. This passage tells about—
- ⬭ puffins catching fish.
- ⬭ puffins digging in the earth.
- ⬭ the colors of the puffin's beak.
- ⬭ the ways puffins use their beaks.

2. Which sentence best summarizes the first paragraph?
- ⬭ Puffins are seabirds.
- ⬭ The puffin's beak helps it catch lots of fish.
- ⬭ The puffin's beak is like a hook.
- ⬭ The puffin's beak has many uses.

3. Which sentence best summarizes the second paragraph?
- ⬭ Puffins dig with their beaks.
- ⬭ Puffins' beaks are very strong.
- ⬭ Puffins like to dig.
- ⬭ The puffin's beak has many uses.

4. Which sentence best summarizes the third paragraph?
- ⬭ Puffins' beaks are greyish brown.
- ⬭ Brightly colored beaks help puffins find mates.
- ⬭ Puffins have bright colors on their beaks.
- ⬭ Puffins' beaks turn red, blue, and gold.

5. Which sentence best summarizes the passage?
- ⬭ Puffins dig with their beaks.
- ⬭ Puffins' beaks help them to catch lots of fish.
- ⬭ The puffin's beak has many uses.
- ⬭ The puffin's beak is very strange.

Notes for Home: Your child summarized key ideas in individual paragraphs and a whole passage. ***Home Activity:*** Talk with your child about the day's activities. Then help your child summarize the conversation in two or three sentences.

Name ______________________________

Phonics: Vowel Digraph *ow*; Diphthong *ow*

Directions: Circle each word with **ow** that has the vowel sound in **grow** or the vowel sound in **clown.** Then write each word in the correct column.

1. Puffins have burrows for homes. They build them below the ground.
2. That's how the babies stay safe from animals on the prowl.
3. In the spring, flowers cover the ground, and the Puffin babies are almost full grown.
4. Puffin babies have to make their way down to the ocean. They follow the lead of the older Puffins.
5. There are some towns in Iceland where children know a lot about Puffins.

ow as in *grow*	**ow as in *clown***
6. ______________	11. ______________
7. ______________	12. ______________
8. ______________	13. ______________
9. ______________	14. ______________
10. ______________	15. ______________

Directions: Circle all the words with the same vowel sound as the first word.

16. town	somehow	cowboy	glow	crown
17. show	frown	blow	yellow	hollow
18. now	known	brown	gown	growth
19. slowly	howling	crow	bowtie	tomorrow
20. owl	crowd	flow	drown	sorrow

Notes for Home: Your child reviewed words with *ow* as in *clown* and *grow*. ***Home Activity:*** Write *clown* and *grow* on two sheets of paper. Take turns listing other words with *ow* that match one of these two vowel sounds.

Name ______________________________

REVIEW

Phonics: Consonants *j* and *g*; *s* and *c*

Directions: Read the sentence. Choose the word that has the same consonant sound as the underlined letter. Mark the space for the answer you have chosen.

1. Not many people have seen Iceland.
- ⬭ cookie
- ⬭ count
- ⬭ place
- ⬭ pack

2. It is a long voyage to Iceland.
- ⬭ good
- ⬭ journey
- ⬭ brag
- ⬭ gold

3. It would be fun to see some pufflings.
- ⬭ safe
- ⬭ ocean
- ⬭ coat
- ⬭ pancake

4. The village children feed the pufflings.
- ⬭ triangle
- ⬭ ground
- ⬭ large
- ⬭ ago

5. They try to save the pufflings from cats and dogs.
- ⬭ shore
- ⬭ candy
- ⬭ cousin
- ⬭ once

6. Pufflings face other dangers.
- ⬭ high
- ⬭ just
- ⬭ began
- ⬭ regret

7. The children race to find the pufflings first.
- ⬭ sea
- ⬭ catch
- ⬭ clowns
- ⬭ busy

8. The children search in the dark.
- ⬭ teacher
- ⬭ distance
- ⬭ she
- ⬭ capture

9. At last the pufflings fly to the sea.
- ⬭ island
- ⬭ nose
- ⬭ cent
- ⬭ country

10. We wish them a safe journey.
- ⬭ good
- ⬭ guess
- ⬭ spring
- ⬭ page

Notes for Home: Your child reviewed words with the consonant sounds /j/ spelled *j* and *g* and /s/ spelled *s* and *c*. ***Home Activity:*** Work with your child to make word pairs by matching words with the same consonant sounds and different letters *(save/cent)*.

Technology: Card Catalog/Library Database

All libraries use a **card catalog** or a computerized **library database** to organize their materials. You can search for a book using the book's **author, title,** or **subject.** When searching by an author's name, always use the last name first, followed by the first name. Each book is assigned a **call number** that appears in the card catalog, the database, and on the spine of the book.

Directions: A database entry for a book on penguins is shown below. Use the entry. to answer the questions.

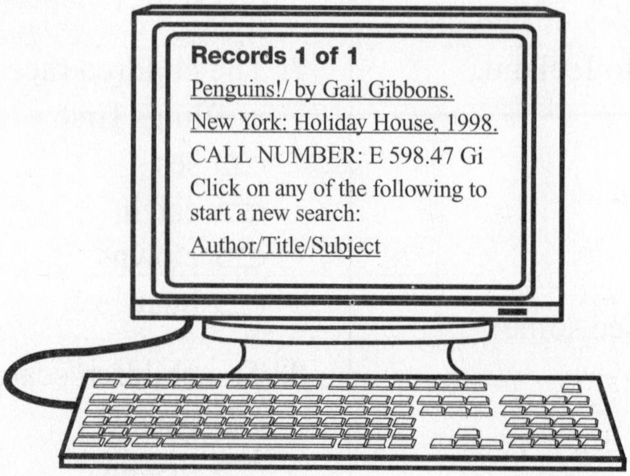

Records 1 of 1
Penguins!/ by Gail Gibbons.
New York: Holiday House, 1998.
CALL NUMBER: E 598.47 Gi
Click on any of the following to start a new search:
Author/Title/Subject

1. What would you type to search the database by author to find this book?

____

2. What would you type to search the database by title to find this book?

____

3. What is the call number of this book? ____________________________

4. What are three ways you can search for a book? ______________________

____

5. Suppose you were writing a report on penguins. Would it be better to search the database by subject using the word *birds* or *penguins?* Explain.

____

____

Notes for Home: Your child answered questions about using a library database. ***Home Activity:*** Visit a library with your child. Have your child use the card catalog or the computerized library database to locate a book by a favorite author or a subject of interest.

Name ____________________

Steps in a Process

- Following the **steps in a process** usually means doing or making something.
- A process is a number of steps that follow in a certain order, from start to finish. Sometimes the steps in a process are shown in pictures as well as words.

Directions: Reread "Cartoon Drawing." Then complete the flowchart below. It describes the process of drawing a pig. Some steps have been done for you. Next to each box in the flowchart, draw a picture to show each step described.

Flowchart	Drawings
Draw a circle.	
↓	
1.	
↓	
Draw two little vertical lines for the nostrils.	
↓	
2.	
↓	
3.	
↓	
4.	
↓	
5.	
↓	
Name your finished pig.	

Notes for Home: Your child wrote steps and drew pictures to describe how to draw a pig. ***Home Activity:*** Help your child make a flowchart to show the steps involved in playing a favorite game or in doing a chore around the house.

Name ____________________________________

Vocabulary

Directions: Choose the word from the box that best completes each sentence. Write the word on the line to the left.

Check the Words You Know

__ authors
__ difficult
__ information
__ libraries
__ museums
__ suggestions

______________ **1.** When we want to learn about Mary Cassatt, a famous artist, we can go to _____ for books about her.

______________ **2.** Reading the books will give us _____ about her life.

______________ **3.** It's not always easy. Finding the right book can be _____.

______________ **4.** The librarian will give us ideas and _____ about which books may be the most helpful.

______________ **5.** Our favorite book shows paintings that can be found in different _____ around the world.

______________ **6.** We discovered that several _____ have written books about Mary Cassatt.

Directions: Draw a line to match each word with its definition.

7. information	collections of books, magazines, and more
8. authors	hard to do or understand
9. difficult	knowledge given or received
10. libraries	people who write books, films, and more

Write a Paragraph

On a separate sheet of paper, write a paragraph about a visit to the library. Use as many vocabulary words as you can.

Notes for Home: Your child identified and used vocabulary words from *What Do Authors Do?* ***Home Activity:*** Look at a favorite book with your child. Discuss where the author may have gotten his or her ideas. Invite your child to use vocabulary words in your discussion.

Name ______________________________

Steps in a Process

- Following the **steps in a process** usually means doing or making something.
- A process is a number of steps that follow in a certain order, from start to finish. Sometimes the steps in a process are shown in pictures as well as words.

Directions: Reread how authors start writing books in *What Do Authors Do?* Then answer the questions below.

When authors have ideas for books, they start to write. Sometimes it is difficult to find the words. Some authors write notes about what might happen in the story. They make lists or outlines.

Some authors who write picture books are also illustrators. Sometimes they sketch as they write. The sketches give them ideas.

Sometimes authors need more information. So they go to libraries, historical societies, museums. They read books, old newspapers, magazines, letters, and diaries written long ago. They take notes. They interview people. They take more notes. They listen and watch.

1. What do authors need before they can start writing books? ______________________________

____

2. After writers have an idea for a book, what is the next thing some authors do?

____

3. What additional steps do authors who are also illustrators do? ______________________________

____

4. Where do authors go if they need more information? ______________________________

____

5. List the steps for writing a book that are described in *What Do Authors Do?* on a separate sheet of paper.

Notes for Home: Your child identified steps in a process. ***Home Activity:*** Help your child write directions for how he or she gets to school. The directions should be in order and numbered.

Test-Taking Tips

1. Write your name on the test.
2. Read the directions carefully. Make sure you know exactly what you are supposed to do.
3. Read the question twice. Make sure you understand what the question is asking.
4. Read the answer choices for the question. Eliminate choices that do not make sense.
5. Mark your answer carefully.
6. Check your answer. Make sure that it makes the most sense out of all the answer choices.
7. If you have difficulty answering a question, you may want to go on to the next question. You can come back to difficult questions later.
8. If you finish the test early, go back and check all your answers.

Selection Test

Directions: Choose the best answer to each item. Mark the space for the answer you have chosen.

Part 1: Vocabulary

Find the answer choice that means about the same as the underlined word in each sentence.

1. Becky reads difficult books.
- ⬭ interesting
- ⬭ hard to understand
- ⬭ beautiful
- ⬭ short and easy

2. Two authors visited Sam's school.
- ⬭ those who draw
- ⬭ people who teach school
- ⬭ people who write books
- ⬭ those who paint

3. Barney has lots of information.
- ⬭ knowledge; facts
- ⬭ make-believe stories
- ⬭ drawings
- ⬭ questions

4. Can you name two museums?
- ⬭ places where movies are made
- ⬭ places where animals live and perform
- ⬭ places where books are made
- ⬭ places where objects are kept on show

5. Tasha went to three libraries.
- ⬭ places where food is made
- ⬭ stores that sell toys and games
- ⬭ stores where clothes are sold
- ⬭ places where books are kept for people to use

6. Mike gave me some suggestions.
- ⬭ things to think about
- ⬭ piles of objects
- ⬭ sheets of paper
- ⬭ large books

Part 2: Comprehension

Use what you know about the selection to answer each item.

7. In this selection, Max is a—
- ⬭ writer.
- ⬭ dog.
- ⬭ duck.
- ⬭ cat.

8. What happens first?
- ⬭ Rufus chases Max.
- ⬭ Two authors write about Max.
- ⬭ Rufus goes to the library.
- ⬭ An author gets a letter.

GO ON

9. The main purpose of this selection is to—
- describe a dog and a cat.
- talk readers into keeping pets.
- tell a silly story.
- explain how books are written.

10. What is the first step in writing a book?
- A dog chases a cat.
- The author makes a list.
- A person buys the book.
- The author gets an idea.

11. Authors show their work to other people because they want to—
- let other people use their ideas.
- make new friends.
- see if people like their stories.
- stop writing.

12. What do most authors do after their books are turned down by publishers?
- They make new dummies.
- They make lists of what might happen next.
- They send their books to other publishers.
- They throw their books away.

13. The people in this selection like to—
- chase their pets.
- write stories.
- receive rejection letters.
- throw stories away.

14. Which detail from the story could **not** really happen?
- Authors get ideas from pets.
- A cat chases a dog.
- Authors gather information and take notes.
- A cat and a dog talk.

15. Which sentence states an opinion?
- "My story is about a dog-chasing cat."
- "His book is more exciting now."
- "They make lists or outlines."
- "They work on their manuscripts some more."

STOP

Name ______________________________

Compare and Contrast

REVIEW

Directions: Read the passage. Then read each question about the passage. Choose the best answer to the question. Mark the space for the answer you have chosen.

What Do I Want To Be?

I can't decide what I want to be when I grow up. Reporters get to meet new people. Doctors, athletes, and police officers meet new people too. Doctors help people when they are sick. Police officers help people when they are in trouble. Reporters get to travel the most, sometimes going around the world. Athletes get to travel a lot too. They get to meet reporters when the reporters want to write about them.

To be a good reporter, I need to be a good writer. To be a good doctor, I need to be good in science and math. Athletes have to be physically fit and have a talent for their chosen sport.

All these careers need people willing to work hard. I'm willing to work hard at my job—or I will be when I grow up a bit more!

1. Who gets to travel the most?
   - ⬭ doctors and athletes
   - ⬭ reporters and athletes
   - ⬭ athletes and police officers
   - ⬭ police officers and doctors

2. Who needs to be the most physically fit?
   - ⬭ doctors
   - ⬭ reporters
   - ⬭ athletes
   - ⬭ police officers

3. Who needs to write well?
   - ⬭ police officers
   - ⬭ doctors
   - ⬭ athletes
   - ⬭ reporters

4. Who gets to meet new people and must be good in science?
   - ⬭ doctors
   - ⬭ athletes
   - ⬭ police officers
   - ⬭ reporters

5. Who helps people who are sick or in trouble?
   - ⬭ doctors and athletes
   - ⬭ athletes and reporters
   - ⬭ reporters and police officers
   - ⬭ police officers and doctors

Notes for Home: Your child compared and contrasted ideas. ***Home Activity:*** Plan an outing with your child. Come up with ideas for things you might do. Discuss the things you like and dislike about each activity. Talk about ways the activities are the same and different.

Name ______________________________

Phonics: Silent Letters
wr, kn, st, gn, mb

Directions: Circle each word in the box that has a silent letter. Then use the words that you circled to complete each sentence. Write the word on the line to the left.

castle	princes	know	story
palaces	knights	mistake	no
wrong	see	listen	write

_______________ **1.** Our class wants to _____ a play.

_______________ **2.** It will be about kings, queens, and _____.

_______________ **3.** They all live in a large _____.

_______________ **4.** We don't _____ much about those times.

_______________ **5.** We will read books to make sure our ideas aren't _____.

_______________ **6.** We will even _____ to a storyteller.

Directions: Choose the word with the silent letter to complete each sentence. Write the word on the line.

_______________ **7.** There was a (bang/knock) at the door.

_______________ **8.** I didn't (think/know) what it could be.

_______________ **9.** I (listened/looked) for a friendly sound.

_______________ **10.** I felt something lick my (knee/hand).

_______________ **11.** I saw a baby (lamb/dog) was there.

_______________ **12.** She had a (hat/sign) on her head.

_______________ **13.** (Printed/Written) in large letters were the words "TAKE CARE OF ME."

_______________ **14.** I found a black and red (knitted/woven) blanket.

_______________ **15.** I (put/wrapped) it around the poor little thing.

Notes for Home: Your child reviewed words with silent letters: *wr, kn, st, gn, mb.* ***Home Activity:*** Work with your child to see how many words with those silent letters you can name. Write the words, and take turns making sentences using each word.

Name ______________________________________

Phonics: Vowel Digraph *ou*; Diphthong *ou*

REVIEW

Directions: Read each sentence. Say the underlined word in each sentence. Choose the word that has the same vowel sound as the underlined word. Mark the space for the answer you have chosen.

1. Most farmers live in the country.
- ⬭ round
- ⬭ rain
- ⬭ run
- ⬭ crowd

2. We wrote an outline for our report.
- ⬭ torn
- ⬭ town
- ⬭ ate
- ⬭ oil

3. Do you like soccer?
- ⬭ young
- ⬭ our
- ⬭ new
- ⬭ bound

4. He ran around the bases.
- ⬭ now
- ⬭ raw
- ⬭ row
- ⬭ soup

5. Our group made the biggest tower.
- ⬭ grew
- ⬭ crop
- ⬭ good
- ⬭ guppy

6. We like to jump and shout.
- ⬭ shoe
- ⬭ shut
- ⬭ owl
- ⬭ hoot

7. They live in a blue house.
- ⬭ mouse
- ⬭ moose
- ⬭ hose
- ⬭ you

8. My dad makes very thick soup.
- ⬭ sour
- ⬭ soul
- ⬭ stew
- ⬭ shook

9. Don't put that in your mouth!
- ⬭ mood
- ⬭ court
- ⬭ troop
- ⬭ sound

10. Tell me about the puppies.
- ⬭ but
- ⬭ tower
- ⬭ before
- ⬭ booth

Notes for Home: Your child reviewed words spelled with *ou* that have the vowel sounds heard in *around* and *group*. ***Home Activity:*** Look for simple words with *ou* in the newspaper or a magazine. Ask your child to read them aloud to you.

Name ______________________________

Schedule

A **schedule** is a written plan that lists events and when they take place.

Directions: Look at the schedule of hours that shows when the Midvale Central Library is open. Then answer the questions below.

Day	**Hours Open**
Monday	10:00 A.M.–6:00 P.M.
Tuesday	10:00 A.M.–6:00 P.M.
Wednesday	10:00 A.M.–10:00 P.M.
Thursday	10:00 A.M.–6:00 P.M.
Friday	10:00 A.M.–6:00 P.M.
Saturday	12:00 P.M.–6:00 P.M.
Sunday	CLOSED

Hours are subject to change for holidays.

1. Does the library have the same number of hours every day? Explain.

____

____

2. Is the library open more hours in the morning or the afternoon? __________

3. If you wanted to do research at the library during the weekend, which day should you plan to go? Explain.

____

4. Which day is the library open the longest? ______________

5. Describe a type of schedule you used and why you used it.

____

____

Notes for Home: Your child answered questions about a schedule. ***Home Activity:*** Share a train, bus, or TV program schedule with your child. Ask your child questions about the schedule. For example: *At what time can you catch a bus going to Ramsey, NJ?*

Name ______________________________

Summarizing

- In a **summary,** a few sentences tell the main ideas in a story or article.
- A summary of a story tells what the story is all about without telling details.

Directions: Reread "To Catch a Rabbit." Then complete the table. Write a summary for each part of the story listed.

Part of the Story	Summary
Paragraph 1 (Wild rabbits . . .)	**1.**
Paragraphs 2 and 3 (Willie was interested . . . /And Willie thought . . .)	**2.**
Paragraph 4 (So, when Mother's Day . . .)	**3.**
Paragraph 5 (But this morning . . .)	**4.**
Paragraphs 6 and 7 (Eva pushed . . . /Willie smiled . . .)	**5.**

Notes for Home: Your child summarized parts of a story. ***Home Activity:*** Have your child use his or her completed table above to help him or her summarize the story for you.

Name ____________________

Vocabulary

Directions: Choose the word from the box that best completes each sentence. Write the word on the line to the left.

Check the Words You Know

- __ business
- __ cheated
- __ clever
- __ harvesting
- __ lazy
- __ partners
- __ wealth

__________ **1.** Farmers are in the _____ of growing food.

__________ **2.** Sometimes two or more farmers work together as _____.

__________ **3.** If they work hard and the crops are good, they will have great _____ .

__________ **4.** If farmers are _____ and let the weeds grow, they will not have good crops.

__________ **5.** Some farmers are _____ and know just what crops to plant to grow the most.

__________ **6.** In the summer and fall, they work very hard _____ their crops.

__________ **7.** If the crops are small, they may feel that bad weather _____ them.

Directions: Choose the word from the box that best answers each clue. Write the word on the line to the left.

__________ **8.** If you were this, you wouldn't like hard work.

__________ **9.** These are people who are in business together.

__________ **10.** This is the buying and selling of goods and services.

Write a Business Plan

On a separate sheet of paper, write about a way that you could earn some money. Use as many vocabulary words as you can.

Notes for Home: Your child identified and used vocabulary words from *Tops and Bottoms*. ***Home Activity:*** Work with your child to write a story about being a farmer. Encourage him or her to use as many vocabulary words as possible.

Name ____________________

Summarizing

- In a **summary**, a few sentences tell about the main ideas in a story or article.
- A summary of a story tells what the story is all about without telling details.

Directions: Reread what happens in *Tops and Bottoms* the first time Hare offers to plant the field. Then answer the questions below.

"So, what will it be, Bear?" asked Hare. "The top half or the bottom half? It's up to you—tops or bottoms."

"Uh, let's see," Bear said with a yawn. "I'll take the top half, Hare. Right—tops."

Hare smiled. "It's a done deal, Bear."

So Bear went back to sleep, and Hare and his family went to work. Hare planted, Mrs. Hare watered, and everyone weeded.

Bear slept as the crops grew.

When it was time for the harvest, Hare called out, "Wake up, Bear! You get the tops and I get the bottoms."

Hare and his family dug up the carrots, the radishes, and the beets. Hare plucked off all the tops, tossed them into a pile for Bear, and put the bottoms aside for himself.

1. What part of the crop did Bear decide to take? ____________________

____

2. What did Hare plant? ____________________

____

3. What did Hare's choice of crops mean for Bear? ____________________

____

4. How would you summarize this section of the story?

____

____

____

5. On a separate sheet of paper, summarize *Tops and Bottoms* in a few sentences.

Notes for Home: Your child summarized a story's main ideas. ***Home Activity:*** Ask your child to retell a favorite story. Then ask him or her to give you a summary of what the story is all about using just a few sentences.

Test-Taking Tips

1. Write your name on the test.
2. Read the directions carefully. Make sure you know exactly what you are supposed to do.
3. Read the question twice. Make sure you understand what the question is asking.
4. Read the answer choices for the question. Eliminate choices that do not make sense.
5. Mark your answer carefully.
6. Check your answer. Make sure that it makes the most sense out of all the answer choices.
7. If you have difficulty answering a question, you may want to go on to the next question. You can come back to difficult questions later.
8. If you finish the test early, go back and check all your answers.

Selection Test

Directions: Choose the best answer to each item. Mark the space for the answer you have chosen.

Part 1: Vocabulary

Find the answer choice that means about the same as the underlined word in each sentence.

1. The <u>clever</u> boy opened the box.
- ⊂⊃ strong
- ⊂⊃ smart
- ⊂⊃ tall
- ⊂⊃ fast

2. The <u>lazy</u> children sat on the porch.
- ⊂⊃ dark yellow
- ⊂⊃ very warm
- ⊂⊃ not willing to work
- ⊂⊃ eager to please

3. They are <u>harvesting</u> corn today.
- ⊂⊃ planting
- ⊂⊃ watering
- ⊂⊃ weeding
- ⊂⊃ gathering

4. Felix got his <u>wealth</u> from his dad.
- ⊂⊃ good taste
- ⊂⊃ looks
- ⊂⊃ riches
- ⊂⊃ clothes

5. Ned thought that Max <u>cheated</u> him.
- ⊂⊃ grew crops for
- ⊂⊃ treated in an unfair way
- ⊂⊃ traded for money
- ⊂⊃ liked very much

6. Tara is a good <u>business</u> person.
- ⊂⊃ kind of machine
- ⊂⊃ house where people live
- ⊂⊃ work done to earn a living
- ⊂⊃ place where people play

7. Jack and Mike are <u>partners</u>.
- ⊂⊃ people who work together
- ⊂⊃ members of the same family
- ⊂⊃ friends who have the same name
- ⊂⊃ people who eat the same foods

Part 2: Comprehension

Use what you know about the story to answer each item.

8. In this story, Hare wanted to—
- ⊂⊃ take care of his family.
- ⊂⊃ work with Bear.
- ⊂⊃ eat the tops of vegetables.
- ⊂⊃ help Bear.

GO ON

9. Which is the best sentence to tell what happens in this story?
- ⬭ Bear got the tops of the carrots, while Hare got the bottoms.
- ⬭ Hare grew corn on Bear's land.
- ⬭ Bear's father gave lots of money and land to Bear.
- ⬭ Hare earned back his land by working hard and tricking Bear.

10. Which words best describe Hare?
- ⬭ sleepy and lazy
- ⬭ smart and hard-working
- ⬭ unhappy and lonely
- ⬭ shy and quiet

11. Why does Hare want Bear as a business partner?
- ⬭ He thinks Bear will work hard.
- ⬭ He likes to help his neighbors.
- ⬭ He knows he can trick Bear.
- ⬭ He needs Bear's strong help.

12. When Bear said he wanted the bottoms, Hare planted lettuce and broccoli because—
- ⬭ he knew they would grow well.
- ⬭ the best parts are the tops.
- ⬭ Bear did not like lettuce.
- ⬭ Hare liked the bottoms best.

13. Which part of the story could happen in real life?
- ⬭ Bear sleeps as the crops grow.
- ⬭ Hare and Bear become business partners.
- ⬭ The Hare family plants crops.
- ⬭ Hare and Mrs. Hare open a vegetable stand.

14. Bear decided to plant his own crops because he wanted to—
- ⬭ save Hare from working too hard.
- ⬭ be Hare's business partner.
- ⬭ have the best parts for himself.
- ⬭ grow more than Hare did.

15. The Hares probably opened their vegetable stand because they—
- ⬭ grew more than they could eat.
- ⬭ wanted to be business partners with Bear.
- ⬭ learned to live happily with Bear as a neighbor.
- ⬭ thought Bear would not grow enough food for himself.

STOP

Name ______________________________

Sequence

REVIEW

Directions: Read the story. Then read each question about the story. Choose the best answer to the question. Mark the space for the answer you have chosen.

Sam the Detective

Sam is a detective. He looks at clues to figure things out. Today, he had to find out what happened to his little brother's teddy bear.

Sam looked in Bob's room. He looked in his own room. He asked his brother where the bear had been seen last. Bob said he had it at dinner. So Sam looked in the kitchen. The bear wasn't there, but Sam did see dirty paw prints. Did the dog know anything?

He found the dog in the basement. His paws were covered in fresh dirt. Sam looked in the garden. He saw a fresh hole. He looked in the hole and found the teddy bear. His brother was very happy. Sam and Bob's mom was happy, too, once she gave the bear a bath in the washing machine, of course.

1. What did Sam do first?
- ⬭ He looked in Bob's room.
- ⬭ He looked in the kitchen.
- ⬭ He looked in the garden.
- ⬭ He looked at a dog.

2. What did Sam do after he looked in his own room?
- ⬭ He looked at the dog.
- ⬭ He talked to Bob.
- ⬭ He looked in the basement.
- ⬭ He looked at the dog.

3. Where did Sam go before he looked in the garden?
- ⬭ to the attic
- ⬭ to the family room
- ⬭ to the dog house in the yard
- ⬭ to the basement

4. What happened after Sam saw the hole in the garden?
- ⬭ He asked Bob where the bear had been seen last.
- ⬭ He found the dog.
- ⬭ He found the teddy bear.
- ⬭ He washed the teddy bear.

5. What happened last in the story?
- ⬭ Sam found the teddy bear.
- ⬭ Sam gave the bear to Bob.
- ⬭ Bob lost his teddy bear.
- ⬭ Sam and Bob's mom washed the teddy bear.

Notes for Home: Your child identified the order in which events happen in a story. ***Home Activity:*** Read a story to your child. Then pick three or four events from the story and ask your child to tell you which of them came first and which came last.

Name ______________________________

Phonics: *r*-Controlled Vowels

Directions: Choose the words from the box that have the same vowel sound as the word at the top of each column. Write each word in the correct column.

garbage	fare	staircase	alarm	bear
hardest	marching	hare	partners	pair

care

1. ______________________
2. ______________________
3. ______________________
4. ______________________
5. ______________________

far

6. ______________________
7. ______________________
8. ______________________
9. ______________________
10. ______________________

Directions: Find the words with the vowel sound in **care** or in **far.** Circle each word that has the same vowel sound as **care.** Underline each word that has the same vowel sound as **far.** Write the words on the lines.

______________ **11.** Hannah and Boris worked all summer in the garden.

______________ **12.** They carefully dug straight rows with hoes.

______________ **13.** They worked long and hard until all the vegetables were planted.

______________ **14.** Hannah and Boris wanted to sell the vegetables at the local fair.

______________ **15.** They would need to hire a cart so they could travel faster.

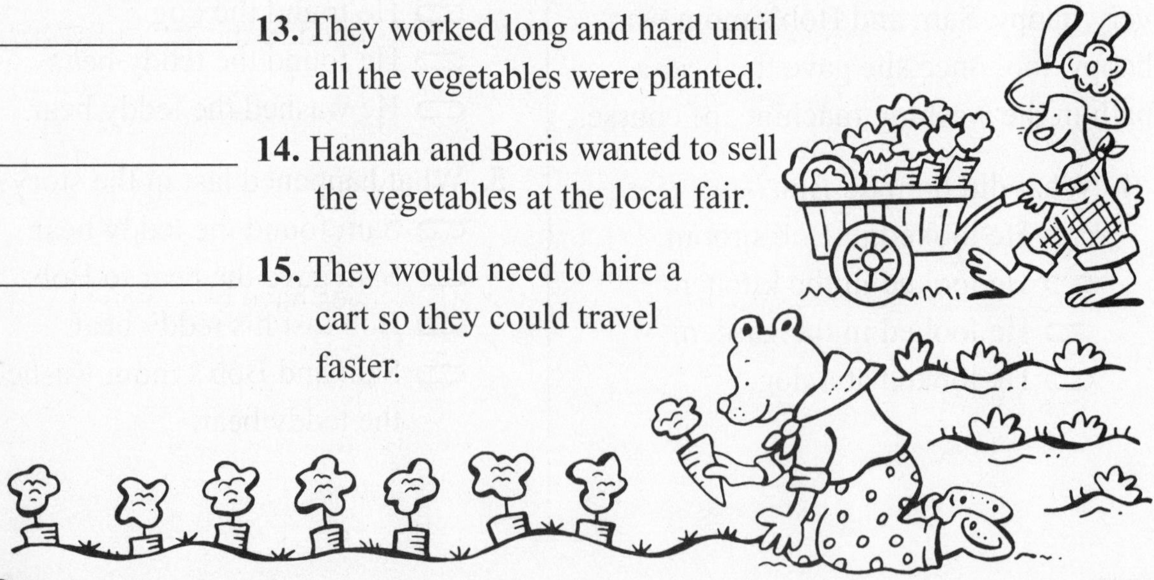

Notes for Home: Your child reviewed words with r-controlled vowels where the *r* that follows the vowels changes the way it sounds as in *care, fair, bear,* and *far.* ***Home Activity:*** Help your child list words with *are, air, ear,* and *ar* that rhyme with *care, fair, bear,* and *far.*

Name ______________________________

Phonics: Vowel Digraph *ow*; Diphthong *ow*

REVIEW

Directions: Read each sentence. Say the underlined word in each sentence. Choose the word that has the same vowel sound as the underlined word. Mark the space for the answer you have chosen.

1. This is my own book.
- bone
- born
- down
- now

2. We walked down the street.
- done
- round
- dawn
- tow

3. The dog growled at us.
- groan
- role
- house
- grew

4. My father owned a grand piano.
- wound
- town
- toe
- dew

5. It is now time to go home.
- grew
- mouse
- hoot
- know

6. You owe me a quarter.
- went
- store
- bowl
- brown

7. Turtles are slow animals.
- show
- sloppy
- sweat
- sound

8. He frowned when he saw the mess.
- owned
- found
- flow
- flopped

9. We climbed to the top of the tower.
- two
- twin
- bounce
- broke

10. The leaves have blown away.
- blew
- code
- lawn
- down

Notes for Home: Your child identified the different vowel sounds for words with *ow (down, owe)*. ***Home Activity:*** Ask your child to write a poem using words that rhyme with *down* and *owe*.

Name ______________________

Questions for Inquiry

Ask yourself **questions** before you read or do research. Look for answers to your questions as you read. You may need to revise your original questions, depending on the information you find.

Directions: Write down two questions you would want to find out about the kinds of shelters used for animals on farms. Then read the passage below.

1. ______________________

2. ______________________

Shelters for Animals

There are two types of shelters found on farms. The first type of shelter is a multipurpose shelter, which means it can be used for more than one purpose. It is built to be a shelter for animals and as a place to store food and machines. The second type of shelter is built only for animals. In places where the weather is cold, the barns are built with insulated walls. In places where the weather is mild, the barns are left open on one or two sides.

Different animals need different types of shelters. Horses live in individual stalls with plenty of space to move around. Mules are kept together in pens. Sheep and goats live in pastures, often without any shelter. In the winter, they live in large sheds.

3. Were your questions answered? If so, what answers did you find? If not, how would you revise your original questions?

____

____

4. Write down another question you still have about shelters for farm animals.

____

5. Where might you find the answer to your question? Think of different sources of information that might tell about farms and farm animals.

____

____

Notes for Home: Your child wrote questions to help set a purpose for reading about a subject. ***Home Activity:*** Have your child write a list of questions of things he or she would like to find out about a topic of interest. Work together to find the answers.

Name ______________________________

Text Structure

- **Text structure** is the way a story or article is organized.
- One way an author can organize the text is to tell things in the order that they happen.
- Use what you already know about story order to understand what you are reading.

Directions: Reread "Puppy Training." Complete the table. Use the questions in the table to help you think about how the article is organized.

Questions	Explanations
What do you learn about in the first paragraph?	**1.**
What do you learn about in the second paragraph?	**2.**
Would the article make sense if the second paragraph came before the first paragraph?	**3.**
How is this article organized?	**4.**
Why do you think it's organized the way that it is?	**5.**

Notes for Home: Your child described how an article is organized. ***Home Activity:*** Read a nonfiction story with your child. Ask him or her to look at how the story is organized. If you want, use this table as a guide.

Name ______________________

Vocabulary

Directions: Write the word from the box that belongs in each group.

Check the Words You Know
__ bounded
__ correcting
__ direction
__ easily
__ guide
__ harness
__ introduce
__ patient

1. fixing, making right, ____________
2. helper, leader, ____________
3. calm, willing to wait, ____________
4. greet, make known, ____________
5. without difficulty, without trying hard, ____________
6. leash, collar, ____________
7. leaped, jumped, ____________

Directions: Choose the word from the box that best completes each sentence. Write the word on the line to the left.

____________ **8.** My dog is always jumping up on people, and I am always _____ her.

____________ **9.** She knows the way home, but when she sees cats, she runs off in the wrong _____.

____________ **10.** She might get lost without me to _____ her.

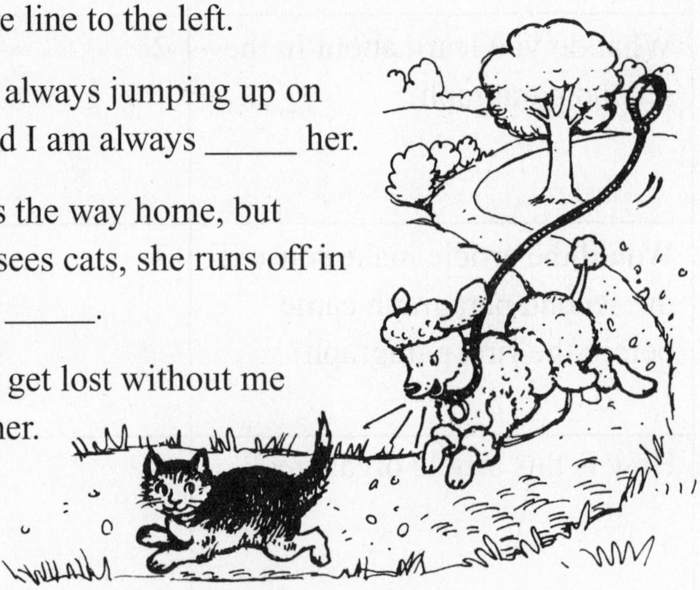

Write a Newspaper Article

On a separate sheet of paper, write a newspaper article about animals that help people. Use as many of the vocabulary words as you can.

Notes for Home: Your child identified and used vocabulary words from *Mom's Best Friend*. ***Home Activity:*** Take turns with your child telling a story about a dog. Let your child make up the first sentence, you say the second, and so on. Try to include the vocabulary words.

Name ________________________

Text Structure

- **Text structure** is the way a story or article is organized.
- One way an author can organize text is to tell things in the order that they happen.
- Use what you already know about story order to understand what you are reading.

Directions: Reread the part of *Mom's Best Friend* where Leslie watches her mom train Ursula. Then answer the questions below.

So I tried to be patient and watched Mom work hard. First she showed one route in our neighborhood to Ursula and walked it over and over. Then she taught her a new route, repeated that, and reviewed the old one. Every day she took Ursula on two trips, walking two or three miles. She fed her, groomed her, gave her obedience training. Twice a week Mom cleaned Ursula's ears and brushed her teeth.

"I'm as busy as I was when you and Joel were little!" she said.

1. What does Leslie's mom teach Ursula to do first? ________________________

____

2. How does Ursula learn a route? ________________________

____

3. What does Leslie's mom do next after she teaches Ursula a new route?

____

4. What other activities does Leslie's mom do with Ursula? ________________________

____

____

5. Reread all of *Mom's Best Friend*. Think about the events in the story. Then, on a separate sheet of paper, describe how most of the events are presented.

Notes for Home: Your child looked at how information in a text was organized. ***Home Activity:*** Ask your child to tell you about something he or she did that day. Remind your child to tell the events in the order in which they happened. Discuss why this order makes sense.

Test-Taking Tips

1. Write your name on the test.
2. Read the directions carefully. Make sure you know exactly what you are supposed to do.
3. Read the question twice. Make sure you understand what the question is asking.
4. Read the answer choices for the question. Eliminate choices that do not make sense.
5. Mark your answer carefully.
6. Check your answer. Make sure that it makes the most sense out of all the answer choices.
7. If you have difficulty answering a question, you may want to go on to the next question. You can come back to difficult questions later.
8. If you finish the test early, go back and check all your answers.

Name ____________________

Selection Test

Directions: Choose the best answer to each item. Mark the space for the answer you have chosen.

Part 1: Vocabulary

Find the answer choice that means about the same as the underlined word in each sentence.

1. Some animals are very patient.
- ⬭ ready to feel great joy
- ⬭ likely to get excited
- ⬭ often scared
- ⬭ willing to wait

2. Cindy bounded into my arms.
- ⬭ crawled
- ⬭ jumped
- ⬭ fell
- ⬭ climbed

3. She won the race easily.
- ⬭ with help from others
- ⬭ for a long way
- ⬭ without trying hard
- ⬭ in a short time

4. She was correcting his work.
- ⬭ making right
- ⬭ drawing pictures for
- ⬭ coloring in
- ⬭ making difficult

5. The teams introduce new members first.
- ⬭ ask to come to a party
- ⬭ make fun of
- ⬭ help others to meet
- ⬭ show off

6. Sibyl changed direction twice.
- ⬭ the way one faces or points
- ⬭ the speed at which one travels
- ⬭ the ideas in one's mind
- ⬭ the clothes one wears

7. The guide led us through the woods.
- ⬭ king
- ⬭ show
- ⬭ follower
- ⬭ leader

8. Sam tugged on his harness.
- ⬭ a kind of clothing
- ⬭ straps to hitch to an animal
- ⬭ a sled pulled by animals
- ⬭ a belt used to keep up pants

GO ON

Name ______________________

Part 2: Comprehension

Use what you know about the selection to answer each item.

9. At the beginning of this selection, Leslie's mom was—
- ⊂⊃ looking for a dog.
- ⊂⊃ waiting for Leslie.
- ⊂⊃ in the hospital.
- ⊂⊃ away from home.

10. Leslie was worried that—
- ⊂⊃ her mom would go away.
- ⊂⊃ her mom would be unhappy.
- ⊂⊃ Ursula would not like her.
- ⊂⊃ Ursula would run away.

11. This selection is told mainly by—
- ⊂⊃ describing events in the order they happened.
- ⊂⊃ comparing Ursula and Marit.
- ⊂⊃ having people write letters.
- ⊂⊃ giving the main idea.

12. Leslie's mother was very busy because she—
- ⊂⊃ had a new dog guide to train.
- ⊂⊃ had babies to take care of.
- ⊂⊃ went jogging with Leslie's dad.
- ⊂⊃ cleaned Ursula's ears and teeth.

13. Mom walked the same route with Ursula many times because she—
- ⊂⊃ wanted to learn the route.
- ⊂⊃ was looking for a better route.
- ⊂⊃ wanted to teach it to Ursula.
- ⊂⊃ hoped Ursula would learn to take herself for walks.

14. Which sentence states an opinion?
- ⊂⊃ Mom and Ursula played every day.
- ⊂⊃ Ursula woke the children every morning.
- ⊂⊃ Every night she slept in my bed.
- ⊂⊃ She is the best dog in the world.

15. What can you tell about Marit from this selection?
- ⊂⊃ She did not like children.
- ⊂⊃ She used to be Leslie's mother's dog guide.
- ⊂⊃ She was a bad dog and got into trouble.
- ⊂⊃ She was a very small dog.

STOP

Name ______________________________

Summarizing

REVIEW

Directions: Read the story. Then read each question about the story. Choose the best answer to the question. Mark the space for the answer you have chosen.

Max the Dog Walker

Max walks dogs every day in New York City. Some days he walks more than twenty dogs, but not all at once!

Most people in the city don't have yards where dogs can run and play. People take their dogs for long walks around city blocks or to dog runs in parks. A dog run is a special area where dogs can run around without being on leashes. Many people hire dog walkers to walk their dogs while they are at work.

Max loves his job. He gets to work with animals. He spends most of his time outdoors. Walking dogs even helps Max exercise!

1. Every day, Max—
- drives around New York City.
- walks dogs in New York City.
- walks twenty dogs.
- exercises in a gym.

2. People walk their dogs
- in the park.
- around city blocks.
- in a dog run.
- around city blocks and in dog runs inside parks.

3. Which sentence tells best why some people hire a dog walker like Max?
- People want their dogs walked while they are at work.
- People like Max.
- People don't like to walk dogs.
- People in big cities don't have big backyards.

4. Which sentence tells best why Max loves his job?
- It pays well.
- He works with animals.
- He works with animals, spends time outdoors, and exercises.
- He spends time outdoors.

5. Which sentence best summarizes the story?
- Max is good at his job.
- Max walks dogs.
- Max has an interesting job that he loves a lot—walking dogs.
- Many people hire dog walkers.

Notes for Home: Your child read a story and identified sentences that best summarize the important ideas in it. ***Home Activity:*** Ask your child to summarize a chapter or section of a book he or she has read. Invite your child to illustrate its important parts.

Word Study: Base Words

Directions: Each word below has a word part added to the beginning or end of the base word. Underline the base word.

1. unhappy **3.** unkind **5.** goodness

2. friendly **4.** mistrust **6.** midweek

Directions: Each base word below has a word part added to the beginning and end. Separate each base word from the other word parts and write each part on a line.

	Base Word		
7. ________ +	________ +	________ =	unkindness
8. ________ +	________ +	________ =	mistrustful
9. ________ +	________ +	________ =	uncomfortable
10. ________ +	________ +	________ =	unhelpful

Directions: Find the base word in each underlined word. Write it on the line.

________ **11.** A dog in our <u>neighborhood</u> had six puppies!

________ **12.** Some of the puppies were <u>friendlier</u> than others.

________ **13.** I picked out the <u>cutest</u> puppy in the litter.

________ **14.** It was black and white and <u>spotted</u> all over.

________ **15.** We put him in a doghouse that we had <u>repainted</u>.

Notes for Home: Your child reviewed words which contain base words. For example, *help* is the base word for *helpless* and *unhelpful*. ***Home Activity:*** Read a story with your child. Ask your child to point out base words within longer words.

Name ______________________

Phonics: *r*-Controlled Vowels

REVIEW

Directions: Read each sentence. Say the underlined word in each sentence. Choose the word that has the same vowel sound as the underlined word. Mark the space for the answer you have chosen.

1. The baby hears his mother call.
- hair
- heart
- cheer
- chore

2. My heart was beating very fast.
- hour
- part
- beat
- here

3. The sea air smelled salty.
- are
- rain
- bare
- farm

4. The barking dogs were very loud.
- start
- beard
- braking
- tracking

5. Elephants have very large ears.
- hair
- hour
- read
- here

6. The cars went down the road.
- fear
- store
- clear
- mark

7. She uses her arms to lift the box.
- chart
- there
- storms
- rare

8. My doll sits near me.
- stare
- dare
- steer
- dress

9. Please sit in the chair.
- cheer
- charm
- bear
- bore

10. It is rude to stare.
- hair
- hear
- start
- corn

Notes for Home: Your child reviewed words with r-controlled vowels where the letter *r* changes the way a vowel sounds, such as *ears, heart, arms, hair,* and *stare*. ***Home Activity:*** Help your child write a story about a fearful bear who hides in his lair.

Name ___________________________

Technology: Pictures and Captions

Pictures and captions give you more information about what you are reading. With a CD-ROM, captions may also give you important instructions about how to find more information or see more pictures.

Directions: The following screen shows information about dogs from a CD-ROM. Use the information to answer the questions below.

Golden Retrievers
Terriers
Cocker Spaniels
To find out more about a specific type of dog, click on its picture.
More Info

1. What do the three pictures show? ___________________________

____

2. What does the caption under each picture tell you? ___________________________

____

3. What would you do if you wanted more information about Cocker Spaniels?

____

4. Why is it important to read captions? ___________________________

____

5. How is looking at pictures on a CD-ROM different from looking at pictures in a book?

____

____

Notes for Home: Your child answered questions about pictures and captions on a CD-ROM. ***Home Activity:*** Look through newspapers, magazines, or CD-ROMs that include pictures with captions. Discuss what information the picture and caption shows.

Name ____

Visualizing

- To **visualize** is to create a picture in your mind.
- You can put yourself into the story or article by using all your senses when you read.
- When you read, use details in the text along with what you know about the subject to see, hear, smell, taste, and feel what the author describes.

Directions: Reread "A Ride to the Stars." Then complete the web. List story details that help you see, hear, smell, taste, or feel what the author describes. One detail has been given.

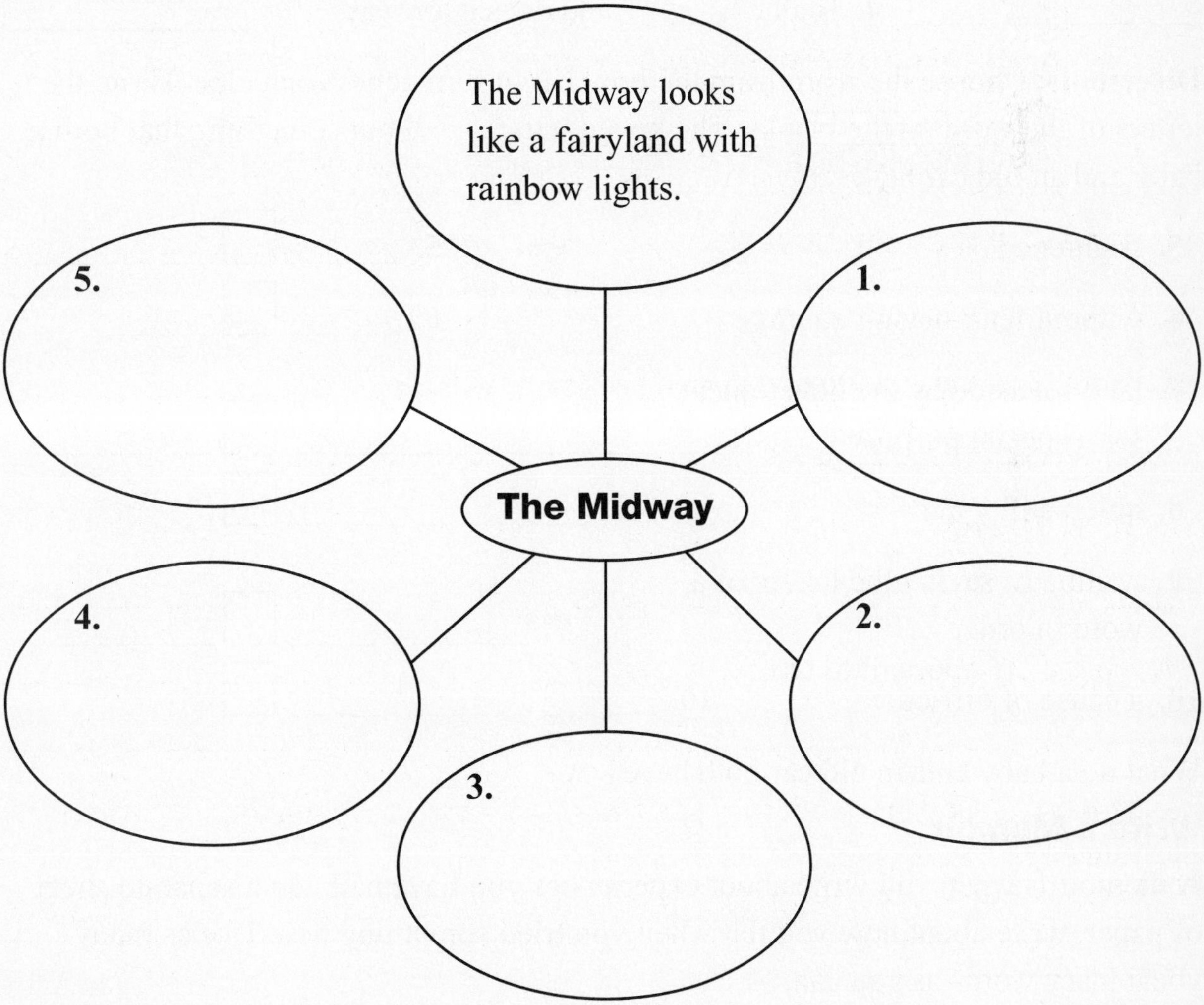
The Midway looks like a fairyland with rainbow lights.
The Midway
1.
2.
3.
4.
5.

Notes for Home: Your child identified story details that help him or her visualize a story. ***Home Activity:*** Have your child close his or her eyes and describe a scene from a favorite book. Draw what your child describes. Then compare the picture with the story.

Name ____

Vocabulary

Directions: Choose the word from the box that best completes each sentence. Write the word on the line to the left.

Check the Words You Know
__ afraid
__ brave
__ reservation
__ silent
__ spelling
__ trouble

_______________ **1.** Our class has a _____ bee every Friday when we have to spell the words aloud.

_______________ **2.** Peter is always _____ he won't know all the words.

_______________ **3.** He would rather be _____ and not have to talk aloud.

_______________ **4.** But he is _____ and does it anyway.

Directions: Choose the word from the box that best matches each clue. Write the letters of the word on the blanks. The boxed letters spell out something that both a baby and an old car have.

5. frightened **5.** ___ ___ ☐ ___ ___ ___

6. without fear; having courage **6.** ___ ___ ☐ ___ ___

7. land set aside by the government for a special purpose **7.** ___ ___ ___ ___ ___ ___ ___ ☐ ___ ___ ___

8. quiet; still **8.** ___ ___ ___ ___ ___ ☐

9. writing or saying the letters of a word in order **9.** ___ ___ ___ ___ ☐ ___ ___ ___

10. a cause of difficulty **10.** ___ ___ ___ ___ ___ ___ ☐

What do a baby and an old car both have? A __________

Write a Memoir

A memoir is when you write about experiences you have had. On a separate sheet of paper, write about how you felt when you tried something new. Use as many vocabulary words as you can.

Notes for Home: Your child identified and used vocabulary words from *Brave as a Mountain Lion*. ***Home Activity:*** Have a spelling bee with your child. Say a word and have your child spell it aloud. Use some of the vocabulary words.

Name ______________________________

Visualizing

- To **visualize** is to create a picture in your mind.
- When you read, use details in the text along with what you know about the subject to see, hear, smell, taste, and feel what the author describes.

Directions: Reread the part of *Brave as a Mountain Lion* in which Spider went to look at the gymnasium. Then answer the questions below.

At recess the next day Spider peeked into the gymnasium. The huge room was empty. He looked up at the mural painting of the western Shoshone people of long ago. They were brave hunters of deer and antelope and elk, just as his father and uncles were today.

At the far end of the gym was the scoreboard with the school's emblem, the eagle. Every Saturday in the winter Spider and his whole family came to cheer for Will and the basketball team. Those players weren't afraid of anything.

Then Spider stared up at the stage. That's where the spellers would stand. He could feel his throat tighten and hear his heart thumping, bumpity-bumpity-bumpity-bump.

1. What picture do you have in your mind of what the gym looks like?

____

2. What picture do have in your mind of what the mural looks like? ______________________________

____

3. What do you think the scoreboard looks like? ______________________________

____

4. How do you think the stage looked to Spider?

____

5. On a separate sheet of paper, draw a scene from the story and tell what details you used to help visualize it.

Notes for Home: Your child described how she or he visualized different story elements. ***Home Activity:*** Have your child close his or her eyes and listen to different sounds in different areas of your home. Have your child describe what he or she hears.

Name ____________________

Test-Taking Tips

1. Write your name on the test.
2. Read the directions carefully. Make sure you know exactly what you are supposed to do.
3. Read the question twice. Make sure you understand what the question is asking.
4. Read the answer choices for the question. Eliminate choices that do not make sense.
5. Mark your answer carefully.
6. Check your answer. Make sure that it makes the most sense out of all the answer choices.
7. If you have difficulty answering a question, you may want to go on to the next question. You can come back to difficult questions later.
8. If you finish the test early, go back and check all your answers.

Selection Test

Directions: Choose the best answer to each item. Mark the space for the answer you have chosen.

Part 1: Vocabulary

Find the answer choice that means about the same as the underlined word in each sentence.

1. The owl was <u>silent</u>.
- quick
- quiet
- hungry
- frightening

2. Tanya finished her <u>spelling</u> lesson.
- using numbers to solve problems
- drawing patterns over and over
- putting the letters of words together in order
- reading words sound by sound

3. She wanted to be <u>brave</u>.
- without fear
- quick and to the point
- easy to understand
- wide awake

4. John was <u>afraid</u>.
- happy
- upset
- excited
- fearful

5. Fran knew she was in <u>trouble</u>.
- something that will not stop
- something that causes worry
- something that makes noise
- something that is cold

6. They live on the <u>reservation</u>.
- place where animals are kept
- forest protected from change
- place used for drinking water
- land set aside by the government

Part 2: Comprehension

Use what you know about the story to answer each item.

7. At the beginning of this story, what would you see if you looked out Spider's window?
- a spider web
- two pieces of paper
- falling snow
- a mountain lion

8. What was Spider afraid of?
- his father's anger
- standing in front of people
- facing a lion
- spelling a word wrong

GO ON

9. What is this story mostly about?
- ⬭ Two brothers play basketball.
- ⬭ Animals help a boy at school.
- ⬭ A boy faces his fears.
- ⬭ Students learn to spell.

10. Spider pretended to be a coyote so that he would—
- ⬭ scare other children.
- ⬭ stay warm.
- ⬭ have a loud voice.
- ⬭ be clever.

11. Spider hoped the snow would keep falling so that—
- ⬭ he could play in the snow.
- ⬭ school would be closed.
- ⬭ his father would not come home.
- ⬭ he could play basketball.

12. Spider decided to enter the spelling bee just after he—
- ⬭ looked at the mural in the school gym.
- ⬭ spoke with his grandmother about coyotes.
- ⬭ watched a spider spin its web.
- ⬭ decided to be brave as a mountain lion.

13. At the end of the story, Spider was most likely—
- ⬭ upset that he did not win.
- ⬭ happy with himself for entering the spelling bee.
- ⬭ tired from studying so much.
- ⬭ sad because the spelling bee was over.

14. Which sentence best describes Spider in this story?
- ⬭ He cannot spell very well.
- ⬭ He does not like school.
- ⬭ He is a star basketball player.
- ⬭ He learns not to be afraid.

15. Next time there is a spelling bee at school, Spider will most likely—
- ⬭ look forward to it.
- ⬭ decide not to do it.
- ⬭ not be asked to enter.
- ⬭ join the families watching.

STOP

Name ______________________________

Realism and Fantasy

REVIEW

Directions: Read the story. Then read each question about the story. Choose the best answer to the question. Mark the space for the answer you have chosen.

Willie and Patch

It was a hot summer day when Willie walked to the lake with his dog Patch. Willie was making up a rhyme. He had learned about rhymes in school earlier that year. "I love to swim in the lake. It's as fun as eating cake," Willie chanted aloud.

"I don't think so," said Patch.

"Don't think what?" said Willie.

"I don't think swimming in a lake is as much fun as eating cake. I don't like the fish in the lake. I prefer pools."

"OK, Patch, we'll go to the pool today. I'll race you." Willie started to flap his arms and fly into the sky.

Patch gave a loud bark and soon followed close behind Willie. Patch won the race by a big splash.

1. Which part of the story could really happen?
- Patch said, "I don't think so."
- Willie flew into the sky.
- Willie and Patch walked to the lake.
- Patch followed Willie into the sky.

2. Which part of the story could not really happen?
- Willie making up a rhyme.
- Willie talking to Patch.
- Patch talking to Willie.
- Willie flapping his arms.

3. Why is this story a fantasy?
- Dogs can't talk, and they can't swim.
- Dogs can't talk, and people can't fly.
- People can't fly, and dogs can't swim.
- Dogs can't swim in pools.

4. A realistic story—
- has talking animals.
- is never about animals.
- tells about something that could happen in real life.
- tells about something that could not happen in real life.

5. A fantasy—
- always has talking dogs.
- is never about people.
- tells about something that could happen in real life.
- tells about something that could not happen in real life.

Notes for Home: Your child identified characteristics of realistic stories and fantasies. ***Home Activity:*** Write the words *Realistic Story* and *Fantasy* on separate slips of paper. Let your child pick one of the slips of paper and tell you a sentence or short story that fits the category.

Name ______________________________

Word Study: Suffixes *-ness, -ly, -ful, -ous*

Directions: Add the suffix **-ness, -ly, -ful,** or **-ous** to each base word. Write the new word on the line.

1. beauty + -ful = __________

2. play + -ful = __________

3. kind + -ness = __________

4. joy + -ous = __________

5. hard + -ness = __________

6. bare + -ly = __________

Directions: Add **-ness, -ly, -ful,** or **-ous** to the base word in ( ) to best complete each sentence. Use the word box for help. Write the new word on the line.

delightful	quickly	marvelous
loneliness	slowly	nearly
mysterious	darkness	quietly

______________ **7.** It was (near) dark outside, and I was feeling lonely.

______________ **8.** I saw a (mystery) figure carrying a package.

______________ **9.** He walked so (slow) he hardly seemed to be moving.

______________ **10.** The (dark) made it hard to see him.

______________ **11.** He put down his package so (quiet) I didn't hear him.

______________ **12.** He (quick) whipped off his hat, and I saw it was my grandpa.

______________ **13.** It was (delight) to see him, especially because he had brought his famous chicken wings.

______________ **14.** The chicken was good, and the biscuits were (marvel).

______________ **15.** With Grandpa there, my feeling of (lonely) disappeared.

Notes for Home: Your child reviewed words with the suffixes *-ness, -ly, -ful,* and *-ous*. ***Home Activity:*** Give your child some base words such as *slow, quick, harm, kind,* and *help*. Invite your child to make new words using the suffixes he or she learned on this page.

Phonics: Silent Letters *wr, kn, st, gn, mb*

REVIEW

Directions: Read each sentence. Choose the word that has the same consonant sound as the underlined letters. Mark the space for the answer you have chosen.

1. Don't forget to write your name on the test.
- white
- ride
- weak
- bite

2. I know how to play the piano.
- wreak
- kick
- near
- cow

3. I like to listen to music.
- ten
- some
- tent
- busy

4. Mary's lamb never comes to school.
- ball
- bulb
- seem
- Bob

5. Look for the road sign.
- girls
- slug
- nice
- clog

6. The snow glistened in the sunlight.
- thing
- please
- light
- send

7. The knight came on his white horse.
- kite
- right
- nothing
- comb

8. We went the wrong way and got lost.
- wing
- ring
- was
- gone

9. I need to comb my hair.
- come
- blue
- brook
- control

10. I will iron out the wrinkles.
- links
- window
- wink
- rink

Notes for Home: Your child reviewed words with *wr, kn, st, gn,* and *mb* where the two letters represent only one consonant sound. ***Home Activity:*** When reading with your child, look for words with these silent letters. Encourage your child to read these words aloud.

Name ____________________

Encyclopedia

An **encyclopedia** is a book or set of books that has **entries,** or articles, on many subjects. Each book in a set of encyclopedias is called a **volume. Guide words** show the first and last entry words on two facing pages. An **entry word** gives the subject of an entry. All the entries on those two pages come between those two guide words in alphabetical order.

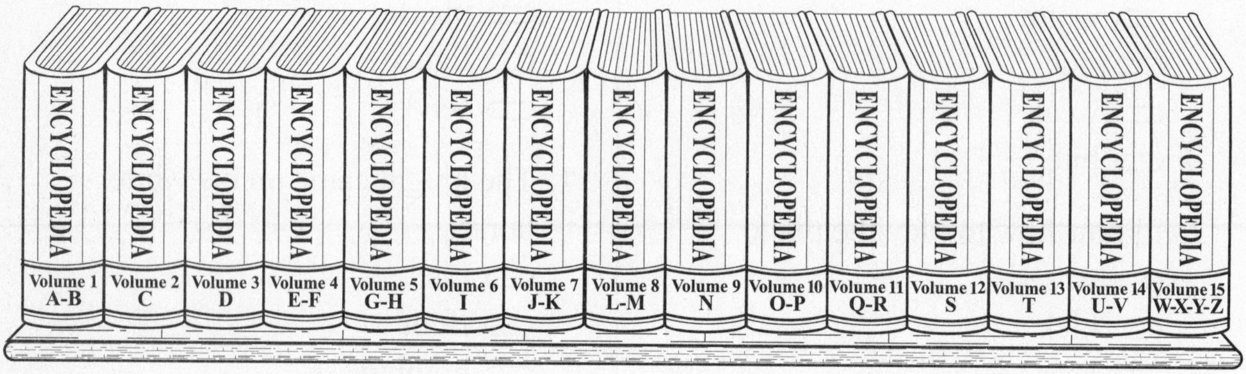

Directions: Underline a word or words in each question that you would use to look up information to answer each question. Then write the volume number in which you would find the information. Use the set of encyclopedias shown above.

____________________ **1.** Where was the first school built in the United States?

____________________ **2.** What is a Montessori School?

____________________ **3.** How many colleges are there in the United States?

____________________ **4.** Who was Horace Mann?

Directions: Read the definition of guide words above. Then answer the question.

5. Why are guide words useful for locating information in an encyclopedia?

____

____

____

Notes for Home: Your child identified words to help locate answers to questions in an encyclopedia. ***Home Activity:*** Work with your child to write a list of questions about a topic of interest. Have your child use an encyclopedia to answer each question.

Name ________________________________

Generalizing

- A **generalization** is a statement or rule that applies to many examples.
- You sometimes are given ideas about several things or people. A generalization might say how they are mostly alike or all alike in some way.
- Clue words such as *all, always, everyone, some,* and *never* can signal a generalization.

Directions: Reread "All About MIMI." Then read the statements below. Decide if each statement is a generalization. Write **No** if it is not a generalization. If it is a generalization, write **Yes** and list the clue word that signaled it.

Statements	Generalization?
The men had all been honored with namesakes.	Yes, *all*
Clarence was named for Mama's brother.	No
All the grandmothers and aunts felt the baby should be named after *them*.	**1.**
There was only one small little girl.	**2.**
MIMI was always surrounded by music.	**3.**
Everyone in the family played instruments or danced.	**4.**
MIMI would shake her rattle in time to the music.	**5.**

Notes for Home: Your child identified generalizations about a story. ***Home Activity:*** Read a story with your child and discuss the generalizations the author made. Have your child tell how he or she knew the author had made a generalization.

Name ______________________________

Vocabulary

Directions: Choose the word from the box that best completes each sentence. Write the word on the line to the left.

Check the Words You Know
__ jokes
__ neighborhood
__ prize
__ problem
__ prove
__ serious

__________ **1.** I like all the people who live in my _____.

__________ **2.** It's a great place, but there is one _____ with living here.

__________ **3.** Every year they give out a _____ but I've never won it.

__________ **4.** It is a very _____ award—no laughing matter.

__________ **5.** It goes to the person who can tell the funniest _____.

__________ **6.** I know I'm funny, but how can I _____ it?

Directions: Choose the word from the box that best completes each rhyme. Write the word on the line to the left.

__________ **7.** At the fair they judged ties, and my dad won first _____.

__________ **8.** But the judges said, "Don't cheer. We see a _____ right here."

__________ **9.** They said, "Don't fool with us! Your tie doesn't look _____."

__________ **10.** So he said, "What's wrong with you folks? Don't you like _____?" And he squirted them right in the eyes.

Write an Announcement

On a separate sheet of paper, write an announcement for a contest. Tell the date, the place, the rules, and the prize. Use as many vocabulary words as you can.

Notes for Home: Your child identified and used vocabulary words from *Your Dad Was Just Like You*. ***Home Activity:*** Have your child make up a story about a silly contest. Encourage him or her to use as many vocabulary words as possible.

Name ____________________

Generalizing

- A **generalization** is a statement or rule that applies to many examples.
- You are sometimes given ideas about several things or people. A generalization might say how they are mostly alike or all alike in some way.
- Clue words such as *all, always, everyone, some,* and *never* can signal a generalization.

Directions: Reread what happens in *Your Dad Was Just Like You* when Peter and his grandfather take a walk. Then answer the questions below.

The two walked through the neighborhood their family had lived in for years. After they had walked some, Peter sighed, "I wish Dad was more like you, Grandpa. He never smiles—he only yells. 'Look at these awful grades, Peter.' 'You never finish anything you start, Peter.' 'Why can't you be more serious, Peter?' He never leaves me alone."

"There was a time when your father laughed and smiled all the time," said Peter's grandfather. "When he was a boy, your dad was just like you."

1. What generalizations does Peter make about his father?

2. What generalization does Peter say his father makes about Peter's behavior?

3. What same clue word signals these generalizations? ____________

4. How did Peter's grandfather generalize about Peter's father?

5. On a separate sheet of paper, give examples of other generalizations in the story.

Notes for Home: Your child identified generalizations in a story. ***Home Activity:*** Look at some advertisements with your child and discuss the generalizations they use. Ask your child why he or she thinks that many advertisements use generalizations.

Test-Taking Tips

1. Write your name on the test.
2. Read the directions carefully. Make sure you know exactly what you are supposed to do.
3. Read the question twice. Make sure you understand what the question is asking.
4. Read the answer choices for the question. Eliminate choices that do not make sense.
5. Mark your answer carefully.
6. Check your answer. Make sure that it makes the most sense out of all the answer choices.
7. If you have difficulty answering a question, you may want to go on to the next question. You can come back to difficult questions later.
8. If you finish the test early, go back and check all your answers.

Selection Test

Directions: Choose the best answer to each item. Mark the space for the answer you have chosen.

Part 1: Vocabulary

Find the answer choice that means about the same as the underlined word in each sentence.

1. Mr. Frick is a <u>serious</u> man.
- ⬭ excited
- ⬭ showing deep thought; unsmiling
- ⬭ angry
- ⬭ scary; frightening

2. Brad needs help with a <u>problem</u>.
- ⬭ game
- ⬭ first job
- ⬭ drawing
- ⬭ difficult question

3. Al moved into the <u>neighborhood</u>.
- ⬭ large family
- ⬭ place where people live
- ⬭ school for young children
- ⬭ place for sick people

4. Randy brought home a <u>prize</u>.
- ⬭ money paid for a job
- ⬭ answer
- ⬭ something won in a contest
- ⬭ lesson

5. She wanted to <u>prove</u> herself.
- ⬭ test; try out
- ⬭ show off
- ⬭ make better
- ⬭ hide

6. Ann likes <u>jokes</u>.
- ⬭ funny stories
- ⬭ games
- ⬭ TV shows
- ⬭ hats

Part 2: Comprehension

Use what you know about the story to answer each item.

7. Which of these happened first?
- ⬭ Grandpa sat on a bench.
- ⬭ Peter broke a purple thing.
- ⬭ Grandpa went for a walk.
- ⬭ Peter fixed his dad's prize.

8. Why did Peter want to move to his grandfather's house?
- ⬭ He liked to run and play.
- ⬭ Grandpa was a good cook.
- ⬭ His father was angry with him.
- ⬭ He did not love his father.

9. Grandpa told Peter about—
- ⬭ a trip to the jungle.
- ⬭ what he was like as a child.
- ⬭ the first job he had.
- ⬭ a race that Peter's father ran.

GO ON

10. What did Peter like best about his grandfather?
- He was easy to talk to.
- He lived far away.
- He liked to take walks.
- He told knock-knock jokes.

11. Peter's father never won a real trophy in the race because—
- he was too slow.
- the race was stopped by rain.
- he fell into a puddle.
- the race was too long.

12. Peter tried to fix his father's purple prize because he—
- did not want his father to know he broke it.
- wanted to make him laugh.
- understood why it was important.
- planned to keep it himself.

13. After his father asked, "Who's there?" Peter most likely—
- answered by saying "Peter."
- handed the fixed trophy to him.
- ran away.
- moved to Grandpa's house.

14. From this story, you can tell that—
- neighborhoods never change.
- fathers don't care about prizes they have won.
- no one ever really wins a race.
- fathers and sons sometimes don't get along.

15. Peter's father probably never ran another race because he—
- found out he was not very fast.
- was too disappointed.
- had to work harder at school.
- already had many trophies.

STOP

Name ______________________________

Context Clues

REVIEW

Directions: Read the story. Then read each question about the story. Choose the best answer to the question. Mark the space for the answer you have chosen.

My Grandpa, the Chef

My grandfather is a great chef. He works in a large hotel and caters many parties. For some fancy parties, he makes elaborate dishes with lots of ingredients that take a long time to make.

When I am older, he says I can become an apprentice and learn to cook just like him. As an apprentice, I would have to work for a long time for other chefs before I could become a chef myself. That is how my grandfather learned in France.

I like my grandfather's hotel, but I'd rather have a small, cozy restaurant of my own. I would create my own recipes and cook them for my favorite customers, who would buy dinner in my restaurant every night. You need a lot of customers if you want to stay in business. My best dish would be pizza—because I love pizza.

1. In this story, the word caters means—
- takes care of.
- cooks for.
- works at.
- runs around.

2. In this story, the word elaborate means—
- hot.
- fancy.
- sweet.
- spicy.

3. The word apprentice means—
- a baker.
- someone who learns how to do something by working for others.
- someone who likes to spend time in restaurants.
- a French person.

4. The word cozy means—
- crazy.
- place.
- small.
- loud.

5. Customers are—
- people who like to eat.
- people who buy something.
- people who like pizza.
- people who make recipes.

Notes for Home: Your child used words surrounding a word to figure out the meanings of five words. ***Home Activity:*** Encourage your child to figure out the meaning of new words using context clues in stories he or she reads. Discuss these words with your child.

Phonics: Medial Consonant Digraphs: *th, ph, sh, ch*

Directions: Circle the letters **th, ph, sh,** or **ch** in the each word. Then write the words in which you circled letters in the middle of the word such as in **kit<u>ch</u>en.**

1. anything	**5.** watch	**9.** alphabet
2. check	**6.** father	**10.** reached
3. telephone	**7.** bookshelf	**11.** photo
4. sunshine	**8.** shape	**12.** peaches

13. ______________________ **17.** ______________________

14. ______________________ **18.** ______________________

15. ______________________ **19.** ______________________

16. ______________________ **20.** ______________________

Directions: Write **th, ph, sh,** or **ch** to complete each word.
Write the whole word on the line to the left.

______________ **21.** Mathew went to visit his grandfa____er.

______________ **22.** He showed Mathew a tro____y that he won when he was Matthew's age.

______________ **23.** His team fini____ed first in a baseball tournament.

______________ **24.** He was the pit____er.

______________ **25.** Matthew's grandpa was a really good a____lete.

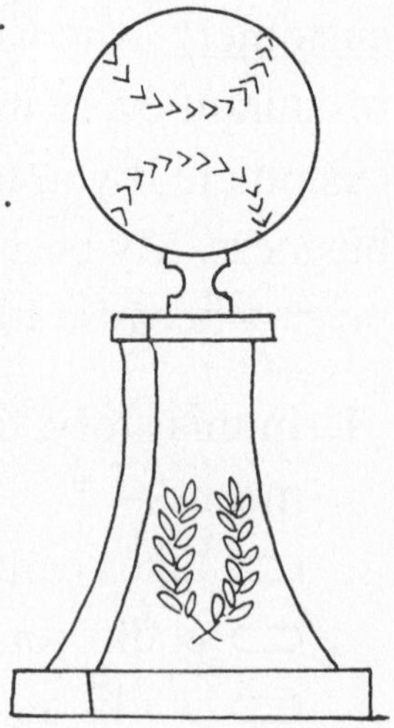

Notes for Home: Your child reviewed words with the letter pairs *th, ph, sh,* and *ch* in the middle. ***Home Activity:*** Have your child change some of the letters in one of the words listed above to form a new word. For example, *peaches* becomes *teaches.*

Name ________________________________

Word Study: Base Words

REVIEW

Directions: Read each sentence. Say the underlined word in each sentence. Find the base word for each word. Mark the space for the answer you have chosen.

1. I built the biggest tower.
- ⬭ bigg
- ⬭ big
- ⬭ bigger
- ⬭ biggest

2. He is running to first base.
- ⬭ ran
- ⬭ runs
- ⬭ run
- ⬭ runn

3. She hesitated before answering.
- ⬭ haste
- ⬭ hesitating
- ⬭ hesitat
- ⬭ hesitate

4. Our neighborhood is very friendly.
- ⬭ neighboring
- ⬭ neighbored
- ⬭ neighbor
- ⬭ neigh

5. We usually have dinner early.
- ⬭ use
- ⬭ useful
- ⬭ usual
- ⬭ usuall

6. My dog is larger than your cat.
- ⬭ larg
- ⬭ argue
- ⬭ largest
- ⬭ large

7. She cut slices off of an apple.
- ⬭ slick
- ⬭ slic
- ⬭ slices
- ⬭ slice

8. A mysterious stranger came to town.
- ⬭ mystery
- ⬭ mysteri
- ⬭ myst
- ⬭ my

9. We went shopping with our dad.
- ⬭ shopper
- ⬭ shopp
- ⬭ shop
- ⬭ shopped

10. I am the oldest child here.
- ⬭ older
- ⬭ olde
- ⬭ old
- ⬭ cold

Notes for Home: Your child identified base words in longer words. For instance, *jump* is the base word for *jumped* and *jumping*. ***Home Activity:*** Look at advertisements with your child. Ask him or her to find the base words in words ending in *-ing, -ed, -ly, -er, -est,* and *-ful*.

Name ______________________________

Evaluate Reference Sources

Directions: Read each situation below. Which of the five reference sources should each person use to find the information he or she needs? Explain each answer.

1. Billy wants to plan a trip to the National Baseball Hall of Fame in Cooperstown, New York. He will drive there with his family.

____

2. Dinah wants to get tickets to a local basketball game. She needs to find out the team's schedule for this week.

____

3. Kojo wants to be sure that he is spelling some words correctly in his article about lacrosse.

____

4. Maria is writing a report on famous women athletes. She has narrowed her choices down to two women, but wants to find out more about each one before she makes a final decision.

____

5. Cory wants to buy new soccer shoes before tomorrow's soccer game. He needs to find a telephone number for Ed's Shoe Store.

____

Notes for Home: Your child identified when to use different types of reference sources. ***Home Activity:*** Discuss each type of reference source shown above. Take turns describing situations where one of these reference sources could be used.

Name ________________________________

Reading Log

Date	What is the title?	Who is the author?	What did you think of it?

Name ____________________

Reading Log

Date	What is the title?	Who is the author?	What did you think of it?

Name ______________________________

Reading Log

Date	What is the title?	Who is the author?	What did you think of it?

Name ______________________________

Reading Log

Date	What is the title?	Who is the author?	What did you think of it?

Name ______________________________

Reading Log

Date	What is the title?	Who is the author?	What did you think of it?

Name ____________________

Reading Log

Date	What is the title?	Who is the author?	What did you think of it?